Mar

The Pocket Essential

MIKE HODGES

www.pocketessentials.com

First published in Great Britain 2001 by Pocket Essentials, 18 Coleswood Road,
Harpenden, Herts, AL5 1EQ

Distributed in the USA by Trafalgar Square Publishing, PO Box 257, Howe Hill
Road, North Pomfret, Vermont 05053

Copyright © Mark Adams 2001
Series Editor: Paul Duncan

A CIP catalogue record for this book is available from the British Library.

ISBN 1-903047-64-1

2 4 6 8 10 9 7 5 3 1

Book typeset by Pdunk
Printed and bound by Cox & Wyman

for Bridget, Jake and Charlie

Acknowledgements

Thanks to Paul Duncan for being laid back but on the ball, and to John Atkinson for introducing me to all that is Pocket Essentials. Thanks - as always - to Julie Pearce, Maggi Hurt and Dick Fiddy at the NFT for ready assistance, and to Tina and Sara for being there when a bottle needed to be bought. Thanks also to my children Jake and Charlie for being available when *Flash Gordon* needed to be watched yet again.

Biggest thanks of all to Mike Hodges for being a welcoming host at his home in Dorset and for talking for hours. I relished watching *Get Carter* time and time again; relived seeing *Flash Gordon* at the ABC in Leicester; recalled meeting Mike for the first time on location with *A Prayer For The Dying*; appreciated his note of thanks when I reviewed *Black Rainbow* for *Variety*; and enjoyed our lunches and screenings of *Get Carter* and *Pulp* when I was programming the National Film Theatre. Cheers Mike! Good luck for the 21st century.

CONTENTS

1. Introduction

It could be argued that after making your debut as a writer/ director with a film as assured and acclaimed as *Get Carter* there is only one place to go - down. For the 30-odd years following his stunning debut in 1971, Mike Hodges has ridden a professional roller coaster, experiencing highs and lows, making some excellent films along the way but also suffering again and again from outside interference. Thirty years on, as his latest film, *Croupier*, receives critical acclaim and audience attention, the phone in Hodges' peaceful Dorset home has been ringing with people from around the world keen to make his acquaintance and maybe even talk movie deals. While Hodges has movie projects in the works, it was interesting to note that the month before *Croupier* opened in the West End, Hodges was directing his play *Shooting Stars & Other Heavenly Pursuits* at a small pub theatre in North London.

The play is part comedy and part drama about - what else? - the movie business, with Hodges happily admitting it is based on his experiences working in the film industry in the 1970s and 1980s. As Hodges wrote in *The Guardian*: 'My litany of failure, mostly at the hands of North Americans, is long. I left one film (*Damien: Omen II*) three weeks into the shoot after - though not because - the producer pulled out a loaded gun during a one-to-one meeting about the design budget. Two of my films suffered drastic re-edits and were stripped of their soundtracks without my consent. On another, I arrived early at a music session only to find the composer secretly recording a truly ghastly secret alternative soundtrack. Betrayal seemed to be a daily event. One film, *The Terminal Man*, was not distributed in the UK at all, and another, *Black Rainbow*, although gleaning great reviews, was given a token UK release because the distributor was going broke. Both films were close to my heart.'

Though Hodges admits to "professionally bruising years" in the period following the acclaim of *Get Carter*, he also takes pride in the tangible accomplishments of the period. Films like *Pulp*, *The*

Terminal Man and *Black Rainbow* might have had little exposure but they remain excellent and provoking movies. *Flash Gordon* was a glossy hit that proved - if proof was necessary - that Hodges could handle a major production. *A Prayer For The Dying*, despite its faults, offers fine performances and intelligent direction. In between his various movie projects, Hodges has always been happy to turn back to his television roots, making many and varied types of productions both in the UK and the US. He even handled the English dubbing on one film (*And The Ship Sails On*) when it meant he would have the chance to work, even tangentially, with one of his heroes, Federico Fellini.

Mike Hodges has never been afraid to try his hand at something different. From gritty crime drama to camp science-fiction adventure, and from supernatural thriller to oddball Mediterranean comedy, his rich and varied filmography cries out to be sampled. As the American Cinematheque wrote when it staged a season of his productions (titled 'Shoot To Kill: The Cool Crimes Of Mike Hodges'): 'There's an elegant mask in front of Hodges' characters that separates them from us: the lethal, impassive gaze of Michael Caine in *Get Carter* and Clive Owen in *Croupier*; George Segal's I'm-about-to-kill stare in *The Terminal Man*. It's the same cool, ironic distance that Hodges brilliantly maintains as director - a kind of Stanley Kubrick meets Jean-Pierre Melville tone that's both seductive and unnerving.'

When Mike Hodges was offered the script of *Croupier* to direct by FilmFour in the late 1998, he hadn't made a movie since *Black Rainbow* in 1991. He admits to being surprised - and pleased - when then FilmFour head David Aukin offered him the project, though still couldn't imagine why. Maybe it was fate - the truth is that Aukin asked one of his key development executives to think of a good director for the script. She went home mulling over the project, and it was during as conversation with her husband that he suggested the name Mike Hodges. "Hodges. *Get Carter*. Hodges. Yup - it could work." And Aukin went along with the suggestion.

When *Croupier* was completed in 1999 the then-bosses of Film-Four were not keen to give the film a major UK release. Maybe it didn't fit in with their schedule. Maybe there was a worry it wouldn't appeal to audiences. Maybe it just didn't feel right at that time. It took the intervention of the British Film Institute to give it a series of screenings in the UK, tied in to a re-release of *Get Carter*. When he heard the news that *Croupier* wouldn't get a proper release, Hodges admits he considered giving up film-making - why would he want the grief? But *Croupier* wouldn't let him. It received a small-scale US release that just built and built with word of mouth and good reviews, making around $500,000 in its first month of release. It was then shown on more than 100 screens and eventually recouped more than its budget at the US box office alone.

FilmFour - now headed by Paul Webster - took a deep breath, looked at the US box-office receipts and glowing reviews again, and decided to take the unprecedented step of reissuing the film in the UK. This time it had a proper press and advertising campaign. The film was a hit. Mike Hodges was back. While it is exciting to think that new projects might be in the pipeline, it also seems appropriate to re-evaluate other Hodges titles, especially *Pulp* and *Black Rainbow*. For Hodges it might well have been an up-and-down career, but there is no denying it has been a fascinating one.

2. The Television Years

Born in Bristol on July 29, 1932, Mike Hodges was brought up amidst the chocolate-box environs (his words) of Salisbury and Bath. His parents insisted that he have a profession, and since he was good at mathematics he studied and then qualified as a chartered accountant. But, aged 22, he opted to go through his two years of National Service, from 1955 to 1957. Whilst on board Royal Navy minesweepers involved with fishing protection, he very deliberately served on the lower decks. He served on board HMS Coquette and later HMS Wave, with the Navy taking him to the Arctic and Iceland during the time of the cod wars. He also spent time in the fishing ports of the UK, an experience that was of great use when he made his movie debut with *Get Carter*. Hodges emerged from the Navy resolved that he would put accountancy behind him and look for a job in film and television.

Hodges initially got a job in London working for Teleprompter, a company owned by film producer Harry Allan Towers, using ancient American television equipment to handle live television shows. The front man was the South African disc jockey Alan Dell. Said Hodges: "There wasn't a vacancy when I was first interviewed. But six months later I was offered a full-time job - £10 a week with no overtime. I became the first teleprompter operator to join the film union, ACTT, and did the job for something like two years, learning an awful lot." For Hodges, working behind the scenes on live television programmes, with a broad range of independent companies, demystified the whole process. "I got to see some pretty bad directors at work, which encouraged me to think I might be able to do it one day, but I also got a great deal of confidence working on the studio floor. Studios can be pretty daunting places when you come upon them. Another advantage with this job was that it allowed me time to start writing."

Hodges met Lloyd Shirley, an executive at ABC Television, and gave him the script for *Some Will Cry Murder*, a television play he had written about euthanasia. Shirley was impressed enough with

Hodges' writing that he sent occasional work his way, and when Shirley was appointed Head of Current Affairs at ABC he asked Hodges if he wanted to be editor of *Sunday Break*, a religious programme for young people. "When I took it over they used to have skiffle bands inbetween religious fodder and it was all a bit laughable," said Hodges. "I changed it radically. I was an atheist, a practising socialist not a practising Christian. The religious advisor was also a socialist, so we transformed the programme into something much more political. Over two years we did some really interesting programmes - again it was mostly live television. A whole raft of television people got started on that programme, including Polly Toynbee, Joan Bakewell and Gus McDonald. It was a fascinating formative television period for me."

In those days Hodges was sharing a flat in London's Haverstock Hill with two ATV cameramen, and had a boxroom which was rented to Robert Stigwood (who would later become a major pop impresario, film producer and manager of The Bee Gees). "The flat later split up and Stigwood, who worked as an agent, turned an actor client of his, Mike Sarne, into a successful pop star," said Hodges. "Stigwood was now in the money, and in 1963 I got a call from him. He asked if I'd be interested in making a documentary about Stephen Ward, a central figure in the Profumo scandal who had just committed suicide. He put me together with Jimmy Hill, a very experienced director who had done some *World In Action*s and numerous feature films, including *Born Free* and *The Kitchen*. We tried to get a script that would stand up, but decided the events were too recent to get any perspective. We dropped the project. As we enjoyed working together Jimmy suggested we do something else.

"I said I had a rather perverse interest in funeral directors. It turned out that Jimmy shared that interest. We went to see Tim Hewitt at *World In Action* and sold him the idea. So we came to make this hilarious one-off documentary entitled *The British Way Of Death*. After that I was asked to join *World In Action*, which was a dream come true. It was a great programme in those days. I never missed it."

World In Action was made by Granada Television and had a strong reputation for radical, and often rather tabloid, journalism, covering a broad range of topics. Hodges became a producer/director at *World In Action* from 1963 to 65, covering subjects ranging from the Vietnam War to the 1964 US Presidential Elections. Hodges produced and directed a wide variety of programmes during his two years with the programme, working on *Radio Pirates* (1964), *Goldwater* (1964), *The Flip Side* (1964), *US Elections* (1964), *The Queen In Canada* (1964), *Vietnam* (1964) and *State Of The Unions* (1964). But it is the *World In Action* that was banned that brings back the most memories.

"I did a programme on Freemasons, which in those days was a secret society," said Hodges. "Nobody in the hierarchy at Granada knew we were making it. When it was completed it turned out that Cecil Bernstein, the financial wizard behind Granada, was a Freemason. As were six others on Granada's Board of Directors. They didn't take kindly to the idea of their weird rituals being aired on television. Cecil's brother, Sidney Bernstein, chairman of the company, flew myself and Alex Valentine, the executive producer, to Manchester. We were taken to the penthouse suite. It was snowing, I remember. Sidney said it was a matter of family, that ran emotionally deep. And though in breach of the company's contract with the ITC he just couldn't transmit it. Sydney was crying while he talked. I remember thinking there was no better example of the power of Freemasonry than that."

Hodges is enthusiastic about his time with *World In Action*, especially because it gave him his first chance to visit the United States. Up until that time he admits he had a fanciful view of the US, seeing it as "the wonderful world of Gene Kelly and Doris Day movies," but his perception was radically changed during his period with the programme.

After two years, though, he wanted a change of pace. "I think there is only a certain amount you can contribute in current affairs and documentaries. You can easily reach a point where it becomes mechanical and you become hard and cynical because that's the world you're having to face. It is better not to continue if that happens."

At this point, Lloyd Shirley featured in Hodges career yet again. ITV's arts flagship programme *Tempo*, which had been started by Kenneth Tynan in the late 1950s, was now wallowing in the schedule. "When I was asked to produce it by Lloyd, it was on at something like 2.10pm on a Sunday afternoon and the budget was a miserable £2,000 per programme. By this time I had become quite expert in 16mm film-making and wanted to extend location film-making to *Tempo*, which had been mainly using the studios. So, over the next two years, I brought a group of talented directors together and we started experimenting. We made a whole series of profiles of people who interested us, including Orson Welles, Jacques Tati, Jean-Luc Godard, Lee Strasberg, Harold Pinter, Alain Robbe-Grillet, Charles Eames and many others. We set out to make each film in a style that represented the subject's work. Each one took on it the identity of the subject. It was a fascinating period."

"While I would direct some of them, I also produced other directors - such as Dick Fontaine - from whom I learnt an awful lot," said Hodges. "It was a particularly happy period, which ended up with *New Tempo* (1967). These were nine abstract films which had an immense impact at the time - particularly in the world of advertising. They were 25-minute-long experimental films. Four directors, including myself, made two each and then the ninth was a compilation of them all. They were called *Information Explosion*, *Heroes*, *Noise*, *Leisure*, *Expendability*, *Nostalgia*, *Violence* and *Stimulants*, and were an attempt to illustrate on film how the world would be changed in every way by the information explosion. Made thirty years ago, they still stand up now.

"They made such an impact that they were repeated at night six months later - which was unprecedented for ITV at the time. I re-showed some of them at the ICA in 2000 and the audience was surprised at how contemporary they were. I am still proud of them. It was a great period of television, the mid-1960s, the freedom we had to experiment was quite extraordinary. That said I don't think Thames quite knew what we were up to at the time."

Around 1967 Lloyd Shirley, who had now been made Head of Drama at ABC, once again entered Hodges' professional life. "I had always been saying to Lloyd that the company should put drama onto film instead of video," said Hodges. "Film was a much better product on the world market. I was arguing on economic grounds, it's the language they best understand. As a result, as a kind of experiment, I got involved with *The Tyrant King*."

The Tyrant King was a children's book written for London Transport. It was about three teenagers who overhear a villain talking about a meeting point; but they can't quite hear where it was. Their adventures take them to all of the major London museums - an educational trip around London through the good graces of London Transport. The production ran in six 25-minute slots, with Mike Hodges as both producer and director. The scripts were written by a researcher on *Tempo*, Trevor Preston, who went on to script UK television productions such as *Out* and *Callan*. Said Hodges: "I proved that you can make drama quickly with film, that you had much more flexibility and could be more inventive using locations than with video in the studio. I also proved that I could work with actors. I'm not entirely sure how it would stand up today, but I proved my point and they now had a commodity that they could sell around the world.

"I now wanted to move onto adult stuff and to do thrillers, which I loved. I think thrillers are like a great conveyor belt carrying you deep into the underbelly of society. Done well they can be like an autopsy of society. Crime is a wonderful way of really looking at what is going on. And so I wrote *Suspect*."

Suspect (1969)

Cast: Rachel Kempson (Phyllis Segal), Bryan Marshall (Mark Segal), George Sewell (Detective Inspector Barnes), Michael Coles (Detective Superintendent Jagger), Jean Alexandrov (Jean Segal), Roland Hunter, Russell Hunter, Dorothy White, Harry Littlewood, Sheelah Wilcocks.

Crew: Director Mike Hodges, Producer Mike Hodges, Writer Mike Hodges, Executive Producer Lloyd Shirley, Designer Patrick Downing, Music Norman Kay. First transmitted November 17, 1969. 80 minutes.

Story: An 11-year-old girl goes missing in a small village, coinciding with Phyllis Segal's husband not returning home from work. While the story follows the missing girl investigation and later the arrest of the murderer, the film's real purpose is to trace the impact on the Segal family. The audience is led to believe that it may have been Mark Segal who committed the killing. In fact he didn't. He had simply left his wife. The film is an autopsy of a middle-class marriage.

Background: Shot as part of Thames Television's *Playhouse* series of one-off dramas, *Suspect* had the original working title of *Daddy*. "It was a very Chabrolesque piece, the nearest thing to anything autobiographical I have ever done. It was moody and set in rural loneliness," said Hodges. "My wife and two children were in the film. We made it in 24 days, and I think it was possibly the first filmed drama on commercial television. Ratings were very good and, again, it sold around the world. I know it was shown on *Iraq Playhouse* during the Gulf War. I know because I was paid a residual of £4.50! With the success of *Suspect*, I went on to write *Rumour*."

Rumour (1970)

Cast: Michael Coles (Sam Hunter), Vivienne Chandler (Liza Curtis), Ronald Clarke, Peter Stratford, Rita Merkelis, David Cargill.

Crew: Director Mike Hodges, Producer Mike Hodges, Writer Mike Hodges. First transmitted March 2, 1970. 80 minutes.

Story: About an unscrupulous showbiz correspondent working for a tabloid newspaper: 'Liza told me her life of sin - a sad, tawdry tale of prostitution, pornography, corruption in high places, sadism and even blackmail, stop.' That is how Fleet Street hack Sam Hunter begins his article on Liza Curtis, supposedly the hottest story of his career. The ambitious journalist is suckered into a scandal story in which he doesn't check his facts. The film opens at Euston Station with a prostitute trying to sell photographs but the hack turns down the snaps because she wants too much money. He later gets a call from her asking him to come and see her. When he arrives he finds the woman dead. This convinces him that the story she was trying to sell must be true, so he starts to make the story stand up - what he doesn't realise is that his own death will finally do the trick. The ending of the film is enigmatic in terms of whether the 'story' was ever actually true, or a fabrication created by the killers - pointing to the fact that rumour can easily become truth.

Background: Following his success with *Suspect*, Mike Hodges once again made this one-off drama for Thames Television's *Playhouse* series. "The film was much more experimental than *Suspect*. I used flash-forwards (shot in the Blackwall Tunnel in London) as an image of a descent into Hell, slow motion, jump cuts, it was very much in the nouvelle vague style. I also used a voice-over to show Hunter's total disdain for the truth. Again the ratings were very good, though I got a terrible hammering from Fleet Street, accusing me of souring the public's opinion of journalists. I wonder if they would say that now?"

In 1997, Mike Hodges wrote in *Crime Time*: 'The hero was a gossip columnist, one of the showbiz rat pack. He is first seen driving a flashy pink Oldsmobile along the Westway in London. In those days a cinema stood behind the flyover. *Goodbye Columbus* was playing there. By carefully excluding 'Columbus' from the shot, my hero is introduced with the word 'Goodbye' writ large behind him. It was a grim joke, an omen. After all I knew it would be 'goodbye' to Hunter at the end of the film. The same bleak humour made me have Jack Carter reading *Farewell My Lovely* at the start of *Get Carter*.'

The television screening of *Rumour* was spotted by the film producer Michael Klinger, which led to *Get Carter*.

3. Get Carter (1971)

Cast: Michael Caine (Jack Carter), Ian Hendry (Eric Paice), John Osborne (Cyril Kinnear), Britt Ekland (Anna Fletcher), Tony Beckley (Peter), George Sewell (Con McCarty), Geraldine Moffat (Glenda), Dorothy White (Margaret), Rosemarie Dunham (Edna), Petra Markham (Doreen), Alun Armstrong (Keith), Bryan Mosley (Cliff Brumby), Glynn Edwards (Albert Swift), Bernard Hepton (Thorpe), Terence Rigby (Gerald Fletcher), John Bindon (Sid Fletcher).

Crew: Director Mike Hodges, Writer Mike Hodges, Novel *Jack's Return Home* by Ted Lewis, Producer Michael Klinger, Cinematographer Wolfgang Suschitzky, Music Roy Budd, Editor John Trumper, Production Designer Assheton Gordon, Costumes Evangeline Harrison, Art Director Roger King. 107 minutes.

Story: *Get Carter* opens enigmatically with a shot of Jack Carter framed in a penthouse window. When an automatic curtain wipes him from the shot the scene switches to inside the room, where London gang bosses Gerald and Sid Fletcher (played by Terence Rigby and John Bindon, whose voices were dubbed to help the American audiences) are watching a series of pornographic slides. Carter stands nearby, helping himself to alcohol. The gangsters tell him they don't want him to go up North because they have connections there they don't want "screwed up," but Carter is adamant. His brother Frank is dead and he wants to be at the funeral.

Carter travels up to Newcastle by train, reading Raymond Chandler's *Farewell My Lovely* in his first-class carriage, and popping into the toilets to take drugs and eye drops. As soon as he arrives in the city he heads to a pub with an extremely long bar where he's to meet Margaret, the woman his brother was seeing. He takes his bitter in a long glass, smokes French cigarettes, as the locals eye him up warily. Margaret phones and tells him she will see him at the funeral, so Carter heads to his brother's house.

He looks around the place, taking down a shotgun from on top of a bedroom wardrobe, before going to see his brother's body, lying in a coffin in a downstairs room. The next day Carter is followed to the funeral by a mysterious Land Rover and, after talking with Margaret, he heads to a local bar with two of Frank's friends and Frank's daughter Doreen. Jack later goes to the local racecourse, looking for Albert Swift, but in the end runs into a gangster he has clearly met before, Eric Paice. Paice is dressed as a chauffeur and Carter quizzes him about which Northern mobster he works for. Carter takes off Paice's dark glasses and comments, "You know, I'd almost forgotten what your eyes looked like. They're still the same - piss holes in the snow."

Paice drives three champagne-swilling businessmen from the racecourse and, from a distance, Carter follows them to a country house named The Heights. Carter climbs a fence, clubs a guard and makes his way into the house, which turns out to be the home of major Northern gangster Cyril Kinnear. While Kinnear plays cards with the businessmen, Carter chats to the beautiful (and clearly drunk and/or stoned) Glenda, who tells him she has met his London gangland bosses. On the wall of Kinnear's sitting room can be seen a Zulu shield and two spears - suggested by some *Get Carter* observers to be a reference to actor Michael Caine's hit film *Zulu*.

After some investigation, Carter finds out that his brother died when he drunkenly drove his car into the river. When Jack returns to his guest house, ironically named the Las Vegas, he calls his girlfriend Anna (who also happens to be the wife of his boss Gerald Fletcher) and proceeds to have phone sex with her while his landlady listens from her rocking chair. A car full of thugs, led by Thorpe, arrives at the house and they tell Carter he has to leave town that night but, after Carter beats them up, he finds out they were sent by a rival Newcastle mobster named Brumby. Carter pays a visit to Brumby in the early hours of the morning. When Brumby threatens him, Carter delivers another of the film's classic lines, "You're a big man, but you're in bad shape and for me it's a full-time job. Now behave yourself."

Carter returns to his guest house and has sex with the landlady. As they lie in bed the next morning and a marching band makes their way up the nearby street, a red Jaguar arrives at the house. Two London gangsters have travelled to Newcastle to take Carter home, but when they barge into the bedroom Carter rolls out of bed and grabs the shotgun. Naked, he takes them out into the street at gunpoint. After getting dressed, Carter heads to a meeting with Margaret, but realises she is the one who told the London thugs where he was and he has to escape them again. This time he is picked up by Glenda, who is driving a soft-top sports car.

She takes him to a meeting with Brumby in the shell of a restaurant he is planning to build at the top of a multi-storey car park. Brumby wants Carter to get rid of his rival Kinnear, but Carter refuses to take the job or the money. Glenda picks him up again, and they go back to her flat and make love. While she is in the bath, Carter starts watching a blue movie titled *Teacher's Pet* and quickly realises that, as well as starring Glenda, the film features Margaret, Albert Swift and, more importantly, his brother's underage daughter, Doreen. Clearly upset, he drags her from the bath, and from there she ends up in the boot of her own car. He parks the car and takes the ferry across the river to find Albert at a bookmaker's. A terrified Albert claims he didn't know Doreen was Frank's daughter (the film implies that Doreen might be Jack Carter's daughter) and says that Eric Paice had arranged the girls for the film. He also admits he had shown the film to Brumby, who had wanted to meet Doreen, and tells Carter it was Eric Paice who killed his brother. With two quick jabs of the knife Carter kills Albert.

Waiting at the ferry terminal is Paice and the two London gangsters. They try to kill Carter but, after he shoots one of them, Paice and the remaining would-be killer head off, but not before pushing Glenda's car into the river - with her in the boot. Carter heads back to Brumby's restaurant and, in a memorable scene, beats up the mobster and throws him off the multi-storey car park (now known as the Carter car park to the locals). Later that night he kidnaps Margaret, takes her to a wood, tells her to strip and then injects her with a drug overdose. Carter telephones Kinnear and tells him he has evidence (the porn film) that would interest the police and, unless he arranges for Paice to be at a specific spot at 6am the next morning, it will be sent to the police. Kinnear goes ahead with the plot, but not before calling a man wearing a distinctive ring with the letter 'J' on it. Carter, though, has lied and the police raid Kinnear's house, where, as well as coming across stoned party-goers and drugs, the police also find the body of Margaret, which Carter has dumped in Kinnear's lake.

Carter tracks Paice to a desolate coal mine by a dark and gloomy sea and, brandishing the shotgun, he chases Paice across the dirty beach, eventually trapping him on a muddy hill where above them industrial skips transport slurry to be dumped into the sea. He forces Paice to drink booze, repeating what Paice had done to his brother, then clubs him to death with the shotgun stock. He lifts Paice's body into one of the skips, and watches as it is dumped into the churning sea. Carter walks along the seashore laughing but, as he prepares to fling the shotgun into the sea, a shot rings out. Carter is shot squarely in the middle of the forehead by an assassin. On his finger is the ring with the letter 'J'. The final scene sees the water lapping Carter's prone body.

Background: On January 20, 1971, not long after *Rumour* had screened, Mike Hodges received a letter from the producer Michael Klinger and the novel *Jack's Return Home* by Ted Lewis. The letter asked if Hodges would like to write and direct a film version. "My career was incredibly smooth - to begin with!" said Hodges. "I read the book, said 'yes' and got on with writing the first draft. I'd never adapted anything before, and stuck to the book extremely closely to begin with. Soon I realised I had to free myself from it and start thinking of it only as a film. I abandoned the flashback elements by which the book is structured, put it in the present tense and rewrote it. This was the draft which was accepted.

"I then wanted to go and look at possible locations. To my horror Michael Klinger said he wanted to come along. On my earlier films I was writer, producer, director and had complete freedom. Now I had a producer who wanted to find locations with me. Up till that time this had always been a private business, a way of getting the creative juices going. I'd drive off alone, in my old Fiat 500, and find them. Now I had Klinger with his Cadillac and his driver Reg Niven!"

Reg Niven, though, had a more lasting place in the history of *Get Carter*, other than the driver on that initial hunt for locations. He was also the body of Jack Carter's brother in the finished film. "Reg was the only person we could find who could lie prone in a coffin," laughed Hodges. "Reg had no problem being inert."

The hunt for locations had a key effect on the final look and structure of *Get Carter*. "I had sailed up the east coast of England during my National Service and seen all of the fishing ports - Hull, Grimsby, Lowestoft. But they had all been radically rebuilt since I'd been there 13-odd years before. For instance, I remembered a pub in Hull called The Albert Hall, a vast rough fisherman's pub with sawdust on the floor, that would have been great for the film. When we got there it had been demolished.

"The book is set in a steel town, but Ted Lewis had never named it. All we know is that Carter changes trains at Doncaster. Well, I didn't know steel towns - but I did know those east coast ports and they seemed equally appropriate. Also the sea would give me another filmic element to play with."

But finding so many of these ports changed from how he recalled them (plus the added embarrassment of turning up to these places in a Cadillac) was disillusioning and Hodges admits he was about to stop looking along the coast in favour of Nottingham. Then he recalled a visit to North Shields on his minesweeper and thought it would be worth a look.

"Before, of course, I had sailed into North Shields. Now I was arriving on land. And to get there we had to go through Newcastle, which I had never seen before. The key to *Get Carter* was finding a location that was hard, that could somehow account for Carter's psychotic behaviour. As soon as I saw Newcastle, with all of these amazing steel bridges, rusty and brutal, I knew Jack was home. And it was my kind of place. It was a working place, not a tourist attraction. It was a place where real people lived. This was where I wanted to make the film."

At this point producer Michael Klinger (as well as Reg and the Cadillac) headed back to London, while Mike Hodges stayed in Newcastle to work on the script. He immersed himself in the city, found his locations and started rewriting the script to incorporate them.

"I remembered that there'd been a well-publicised murder case some years before. A guy had been found in a Jaguar car, shot to death, under a bridge close to a club called La Dolce Vita. So I started investigating the story. A hit man, like Jack Carter, had been brought up from London to kill this guy. It was all linked to slot machine rip-offs in working men's clubs. The operation was run by two brothers, one was named Vincent Lander. The more I researched the more I incorporated the story as background into the film.

"When I was going through the press cuttings, I found one that said Lander had this incredible house (Dryderdale Hall, Hamsterley) and noticed it had been put up for sale because he and his family had done a runner! I rang the estate agents - it was still on the market - saw it and thought it was amazing. This became the house where Kinnear, John Osborne's character, lives. It had a lake down below the house and, of course, all these elements I started weaving into the script. The lake for example, is where Carter dumps Margaret's body.

"The place had very unpleasant vibes - no wonder it was still on the market after three years - but it was great for the film. But it wasn't just locations that came from my research. There's a tracking shot outside the house of all the party-goers lined up after the police raid. An incredible array of faces. Well, most of those faces used to attend the parties at Lander's home."

Many other elements crept into the film due to Hodges' initial stay there. The ferry scene was never in the initial script, and he discovered the girls' band with the drum majorettes, which also found a place in the story. "The film was made in a white heat. Fast and intense. I thought film-making would always be like this. Was I wrong! When I look back, I am astonished at what we achieved.

"I must have had a lot of 'chutzpah' for a first-time director. I would never shoot until I was ready. When I first found the beach location for the film's final sequence it was enveloped in this amazingly atmospheric fog, a sea fret. With that black water it looked extraordinary. But on the day we went to shoot it was a bright sunny day and I was heartbroken. I just walked off along the beach - some of the crew sort of followed but soon gave up. I vanished behind a far-off bend in the cliff face. Somehow I had to clear my head of what I had initially envisaged and rethink the entire sequence. I was in despair - I knew it would look almost glamorous in that bright sunshine.

"I sat there for an hour or more... then I looked up and it had started clouding over. I walked back and we started work. I don't know how I had such courage to hold things up that long - the suits didn't look happy.

"I was also very lucky in that Michael Caine trusted me. He is in virtually every scene and he trusted me even when there were complicated set-ups. I felt completely free with him and felt I could ask him to do whatever I wanted."

According to Hodges, Michael Caine got involved with the project after completion of the first draft. "His name was certainly never mentioned to begin with. At an early stage I was thinking of Ian Hendry, an actor I had always loved, to play Carter. I just never thought that someone like Michael Caine would want to play such a shit.

"Clearly, a star brings something else to a film. When Michael came on board, I realised that the film's reality had to be jacked up several notches because the character of Carter would become much more iconic than I had originally anticipated. By the time we went up North Caine was on board, much to my surprise, and delight."

Even at the very earliest stages of filming - and remember the whole shoot took less than 40 days on a modest budget of around £750,000 - Hodges says he felt they were making something special. "I shot going up to Newcastle on the train, but because of the cramped circumstances I wasn't able to get behind the camera.

24

Our first shot in Newcastle - which was I suppose our first *real* shot - was in the long bar (right after Carter's arrival in the city). This was the first time I had a chance to look through the camera. I had this shot lined up where Carter comes in and we pull back to take in the whole bar and see all of the local characters. Then there is a phone call for him, and he comes up the bar and fills the whole frame. I realised then that this was a whole other ball game - I hadn't worked with a star before - and they are something else."

Also worth watching out for in that scene in the long bar is the elderly extra who raised a pint glass to his mouth shortly after Carter has taken the phone call. He has five fingers and a thumb, a fact that, as Michael Caine takes delight in pointing out, is rarely spotted by film fans. Key locations used include Newcastle's Tyne Bridge, the ferry terminal at Wallsend (where the shoot-out takes place), the Newcastle Swing Bridge (where Carter buys drugs), Dawdon Colliery and the Hawthorn Leslie Shipyard. Frank's house was (ironically) on Frank Street, Benwell, while the Las Vegas guest house where Jack stays was on Coburg Street, Gateshead. The final scene was shot at Blackhall Colliery on the coast between Seaham and Hartlepool.

Caine, speaking on the DVD release of *Get Carter*, also sensed how special the character of Carter would be: "I had wanted to make it because, at that time, British gangster films always assumed that British gangsters were either stupid, silly or funny, and I knew from my background that they were none of these three."

Mike Hodges added: "I think I also caught the city on the cusp. In the late 1960s the face of Britain was changing rapidly and I got to Newcastle just before it happened there. The Scotswood Road, where those terraced houses are, were in fact unoccupied and high-rise flats were due to be built. We renovated one and made it Frank's home.

"I think with *Get Carter* we caught this sense of loss - this sense that the idealism of the 1960s was over - and that a grimmer reality was about to hit the country. Rampant materialism was underway.

We sensed that what was going to replace that 1960s optimism was not going to be pleasant."

At the time that the film was released audiences had been partly primed for the level of violence that *Get Carter* offered. Films like *Straw Dogs* and *Clockwork Orange* had quite recently been on the screens, and *Get Carter* wasn't in the same league when it came to their extremes of violence. "I think that *Get Carter* isn't that different to a Jacobean tragedy," said Hodges. "The body count is high, but while it is hard and violent, it is acceptable. There is a sort of morality attached to revenge - you are on the side of the avenger, even though you are scared shitless of him and loath him, he is justified in a way we all seem to understand.

"Also there are redeeming moments, gentle moments, where Michael is just brilliant. In the scene where he is returning on the ferry, he looks at a mother and her two children and somehow conveys to you that he knows that he is abnormal, sick and is never going to enjoy a normal existence like the family he's looking at. He knows that all his fantasies of escaping to South America are just that, fantasies. Another moment is when Glenda, in the boot of her car, drowns. Another simple look underlines the remorseless game that life is."

The soundtrack by Roy Budd also continues to receive acclaim. Although Hodges had seen Budd play before he made the film, it was producer Michael Klinger who suggested Budd should write the music. Because money was tight, very few musicians were actually used in the recording process. In an interview Hodges described how he likes to use music in a very minimal way: "The *Get Carter* title sequence is a good example. Jazzy music for the journey up to the North, but within what Roy had written I heard these simple chords. I love simple musical statements that can be repeated unobtrusively. I asked Roy to pluck this plain touching theme from the title music so that we could use it throughout the film. It's the first sound you hear in the film, and the last, you hear it again when he finds his brother in the coffin, you hear it a moments when the story calls for it. My main contribution to the film score was to separate that musical phrase and use it where necessary."

Mike Hodges admits to still being surprised - and pleased - that *Get Carter* continues to have a popularity and resonance with audiences. "It has a timeless quality about it. The wardrobe doesn't even seem to have dated. It is amazing how it works for young people - but there you are - I'm not going to grumble." Hodges received a one-off payment of £7,000 to write and direct *Get Carter*, and therefore has never benefited financially from the film's continued popularity and revivals both on the big screen, video and DVD. One could easily imagine how he might have reason to grumble!

Get Carter was remade as a blaxploitation film titled *Hit Man* in 1972, starring Pam Grier and Bernie Casey, and shot in Los Angeles. Another remake, made in 2000, starred Sylvester Stallone as a slightly more tender Carter, and also had a role for Michael Caine, this time taking on the Brumby role. The new version, directed by Stephen Kay, also starred Miranda Richardson, Rachel Leigh Cook, Alan Cumming and Mickey Rourke. The film made little impact on its US release, and went straight to video/DVD in the UK. Hodges, naturally enough, thinks that the notion of remaking *Get Carter* was a strange one, especially when it came to casting Stallone in the role of Jack Carter.

Themes/Subtext: There is a brutal honesty about *Get Carter* that sets it apart from other crime films. Yes, people get killed, but the violence is never wallowed in - it is dealt with and then left. At only one point does Jack Carter seem to enjoy his violence - remember, he is a professional, he is just doing his job - and that is in the final scenes when he kills Paice. He laughs as he walks along the beach, only to be shot by an assassin using a rifle with a telescopic sight. For writer/director Mike Hodges, *Get Carter* offered him the chance to embrace two of his fascinations: crime stories and social politics. Just as the film's violence is honest, so is the depiction of Newcastle - a tough Northern city ill at ease with the softer themes of the swinging 1960s and ripe to fall into the decay of the more brutal 1970s. Forget the colourful and swirling excesses of 1960s crime-caper films, the world of *Get Carter* is dark, murky and seedy. Hodges takes pride in using real people (or rather local extras rather than imported actors) in the bar-room scenes, and takes time to tour round the grim house Carter's brother lived in. Hodges manages to fit in his political messages dealing with the bleak life of the people in the city while also making great use of spectacular locations. And, as crime films go, this tale of revenge is rarely equalled. As writer Barry Gifford (screenwriter of David Lynch's *Wild At Heart*) wrote in his book *The Devil Thumbs A Ride And Other Unforgettable Films*: '*Get Carter* is the movie Peckinpah's version of Jim Thompson's *The Getaway* should have been.' He added: 'Hodges has the action raw and quick; Carter's either fucking, shooting, throwing someone off a roof, or observing. You can see his brain registering and computing and plotting. We don't like Carter - he's a sociopathic, perverse murderer - but we respect his lack of pretence. He may not like himself, either, but he's got his self-respect. Life is for shit, he seems to be thinking, but there's a certain fascination in watching people try to wipe it off.'

The Verdict: It was recently hailed by *Hotdog* magazine as the best British movie ever, while *The Independent* dubbed it 'the best British gangster movie ever.' The British Film Institute rated it 16th in its list of the 100 best British films, and in perhaps the greatest tribute, *Loaded* magazine serialised it in comic-strip form. *Get Carter* has had a lasting impact on the British movie scene. It remains the benchmark by which any British-made crime film is judged and, considering it was a debut movie by writer/director Mike Hodges, it is a remarkable, and quite perfect, film. Forget Michael Caine's Oscars for the likes of *Hannah And Her Sisters* and *The Cider House Rules*, as Jack Carter he gives his best ever performance. For many film-goers he will always be associated with the character of Jack Carter - in a black Mac and casually carrying a shotgun. It is one of those rare films when all of the moviemaking elements - script, direction, music, performances, locations, editing and cinematography - all fit perfectly together. One of the best.

4. Manipulation And Pulp

The Frighteners: The Manipulators (1971)

Cast: Stanley Lebor (Irving Sokolsky), Brian Grellis (Marty Smith), Bryan Marshall (Adrian Wills), David Sands (David Stanley), Kara Wilson (Pat Stanley), David Healy (Frank Mancha),

Crew: Director Mike Hodges, Writer Mike Hodges, Producer Geoffrey Hughes, Executive Producer Peter Wildewood, Photography Tony Mander, Sound Alan Mills, Editor Gene Ellis, Designer John Wood. LWT. 26 minutes.

Story: The film opens with the delivery of meat carcasses to a butcher's shop. A man drops the meat off and proceeds upstairs to join a colleague. These are two undercover agents who are positioned in a single room with a brief to watch the building opposite. Their job is to destroy the lives of the couple and a child across the road - making anonymous phone calls, delivering a fake letter which implies a love affair and recording all that happens with the family. The couple's life gets more and more troubled, but then the watchers observe horrific happenings, as the man appears to kill his wife and child. At this point, one of the agents stands up and says that they cannot continue. The twist of the story then kicks in… The whole thing is a training exercise and the agent who says he cannot continue has failed and therefore has to be killed. The film ends with the man's body being taken away in the form of the carcass which was delivered at the beginning of the story.

Background: "In some ways the success of *Get Carter* frightened the life out of me," said Hodges. "Because all of my work until then had been for television, I had never before seen the effect a film *I'd* made had on a thousand people sitting in a Leicester Square cinema. I found it scary witnessing the power of my work in public. *The Manipulators*, in an odd kind of way, was a reaction to *Get Carter*. It is a film about emotional manipulation. It was shot in Portobello Road above a butcher's shop and pretty much takes place in one room. It is a very strange, cold piece. I was told that Michael Caine was rather upset that I did a television piece having made the break into features. I puzzled him, I think, in the way I wanted to do things.

Themes/Subtext: *The Manipulators* is a fascinating short film with a twist you don't see coming. The paranoia is well handled and in that sense it feels a remarkably contemporary film despite having been made in 1971. The character David Stanley (one of those *being* observed) is a student at a local college studying Pavlovian theory, and Hodges uses the film to explore Pavlov's theories, examining how people respond when placed in certain circumstances and under extreme conditions. Though you don't know it until the end, it is about various people having to pass tests and prove themselves, but it also flags up a concern about security services observing ordinary people and fits quite neatly into the Big Brother worries. As with *Get Carter* the setting is seedy - the watchers watch from a grim room above a butcher's shop, and the 'ordinary' people opposite are a young couple with no money and lots of problems - and the solutions are simple and brutal.

Pulp (1972)

Cast: Michael Caine (Mickey King), Mickey Rooney (Preston Gilbert), Lionel Stander (Ben Dinuccio), Lizabeth Scott (Princess Betty Cippola), Nadia Cassini (Liz Adams), Dennis Price (Mysterious Englishman), Al Lettieri (Miller), Leopoldo Trieste (Marcovic).

Crew: Director Mike Hodges, Writer Mike Hodges, Producer Michael Klinger, Cinematographer Ousam Rawi, Editor John Glen, Production Designer Patrick Downing, Costumes Gitt Magrini, Art Director Darrell Lass. 92 minutes.

Story: *Pulp* is the story of successful pulp book writer Mickey King (obviously based on Mickey Spillane), whose classic titles include *The Organ Grinder* and *My Gun Is Long*. He has also written under the pseudonyms Guy Strange, Paul R Cumming, Les Behan, OR Gan and S Odomy. At the start of the film, he delivers his latest opus to the busy typing pool where rows of young women listen to his purple semi-pornographic prose through ear-phones and type it up.

Mickey, who also narrates the story, is summoned to ghost-write the biography/memoirs of Preston Gilbert, a former star of Hollywood gangster films now in retirement in the same Mediterranean country as Mickey. After a longwinded and secretive journey, during which he has a brush with a cross-dressing hit man who likes reading the novels of Ross Macdonald, Mickey is finally led to the diminutive Gilbert by his hulky right-hand man Ben Dinuccio.

Mickey is initially intrigued by the fast-talking Gilbert but he rethinks matters when he suddenly finds his new employer assassinated by a man disguised as a priest and becomes a target himself. Gilbert had been involved in a sex scandal which had been covered because other powerful people were implicated. Now someone believes that the one-time star has passed on details of the scandal to Mickey. Now he must investigate to save himself. He manages to find the truth behind the plot and even dodges another assassination attempt, which leaves his would-be killer dead (Mickey eulogises over the corpse, "Remember that thou art pulp, and unto pulp thou shalt return"), but Mickey is wounded in the leg and finds himself the unwilling guest of the political leader of the country's New Front party. He ends up stuck in a luxury house, a cosseted prisoner who spends his time writing a pulp novel no one will read.

Background: About a year after Hodges had finished making *Get Carter* he started on *Pulp* (which had the working title *Memoirs Of A Ghostwriter*), again to star Michael Caine and be produced by Michael Klinger. Said Hodges, "I found the script for *Pulp* somewhat difficult to write, but I had enjoyed working with Michael Caine and it had been a successful partnership, so I was keen to work with him again. Although *Pulp* is located in a very different environment to Newcastle, in fact the story is very similar to *Get Carter*. Again, it is about the abuse of a young girl and about my preoccupation with people in positions of power not

31

being answerable. It's the same story but treated in a completely different, comedic way.

"Look carefully at *Pulp* and you'll see that it's actually a serious film. Originally, I was going to shoot it in Italy because the backstory partly stemmed from what was happening there. In the recent local elections there had been a significant rise in the fascism vote. For me that was totally incomprehensible. Having been brought up during the war it was unthinkable for anybody to vote fascist. How naive I was!"

Hodges made plans to film in Italy. "But when we got to grips with Italy, at every location we wanted to use we had to make a deal with the Mafia. I called up Michael Klinger and said that I thought we would be taken to the cleaners. I suggested we pull out and shoot the whole film in Malta.

"I knew Malta well. I had a house there at the time. We only had four weeks before we had to start shooting and Klinger was brave to okay the switch. We had an Italian production manager in place, and a wonderful Italian costume designer, Gitt Magrini. She had worked on Bertolucci's *Il Conformista*, and now they all had to come to Malta."

Hodges admits that the process of writing *Pulp* was a difficult one. "*Suspect* and *Rumour* were also original scripts but they were quite straightforward narrative films, whereas with *Pulp* I was trying to do something else. I admit to being very influenced by the John Huston film *Beat The Devil*, which is a strange piece with a remarkable atmosphere, written on the hoof by Truman Capote. He didn't find it easy either.

"I did a great deal of research into the current state of Italian fascism. I visited Mussolini's tomb - a shop there illegally sold photos of Il Duce, and even LPs of his speeches. At the end of *Pulp* you'll see there's a jukebox outside Mickey Rooney's mausoleum. It's almost exactly the same as the one in front of Mussolini's tomb. There you just pushed a button and you heard segments from his speeches. In my film there is a scene where the leader of the New Front party is out canvassing. All these balloons go up, and you hear a speech coming over his tannoy - that was Mussolini. The film never played in Italy so the joke has probably gone totally unnoticed."

Although he would love to have had the chance to re-edit *Pulp*, Hodges is extremely happy with Michael Caine's performance. "There are parts of *Pulp* I would like to tighten up. But I think Michael is as excellent in it as he is in *Get Carter*. He played the character seedy and overweight, and his voice-over is brilliant."

Pulp also features the more idiosyncratic casting of two Hollywood legends, Mickey Rooney and Lizabeth Scott, as well as character actor Lionel Stander and great British actor Dennis Price, appearing in his last film. "Working with Mickey Rooney was extraordinary," said Hodges. "I had a terrible fight with UA to approve him. The character had to be tiny like Mussolini and Hitler, and also like many gangster stars, Cagney for example. A lot of the jokes stemmed from Gilbert's size.

"Mickey Rooney was out of fashion in those days, but I insisted he was the only person to play the role. UA wanted all sorts of strange people. The weirdest was Victor Mature - I pointed out that he was six foot something.

"I got my way in the end. Mickey was strange - we never, ever talked about the role. He just turned up, put his wardrobe on and did it. I had written a pretty monstrous character, but Mickey made him more monstrous - and I was delighted. I felt a bit sensitive about the role because, in many ways, it was near the bone for him. I learned very rapidly that you had to always shoot him in rehearsal because he would never do the same thing twice. I also learnt that he was exhausting to work with. For example, when you were doing matching close-ups with other actors Mickey would be tap-dancing or pretending to play the drums.

"Lizabeth Scott was equally exhausting, but in a completely different way. She hadn't made a film in something like 15 years and I had to talk her into coming back. She was very nervous and it was demanding to keep her confidence fired up. Certainly casting her was a reference back to those classic Bogart films. She, like Rooney, was just terrific."

Pulp had largely positive reviews when released, but made little impact at the box office in the UK. "In the US it had a premiere in Philadelphia with the whole red carpet thing, but it just died. Then a new cinema in New York, whose policy was to show lost films, chose *Pulp* as its first title, but only for a week. It had rave reviews across the board, but when they came out the film was running nowhere. The distributors rushed around trying to find venues but by then the window had closed."

Themes/Subtext: With his last four projects all explicitly crime related, it is easy to see why Mike Hodges sought contrast by using humour in *Pulp*. However, he stayed true to his love for crime fiction, and combined pulp noir with clever laughs. He also clearly liked shooting in the sunshine of the Mediterranean rather than the grim UK locations of his previous films. Again, though, Hodges' political views are to the fore, and at its heart the film is about the horrors and seductiveness of fascism, dealing with power, exploitation and corruption. The laughs come mainly in the early sections of the film (and there are often very clever and witty laughs to be had) before Caine's character slowly comes under the total control of others. *Pulp* remains perhaps Hodges' lightest film (despite the fact that purer comedies were to come later) in terms of his ability to use humour to deal with political points.

The Verdict: For any director, the follow-up film is probably the hardest to get right. *Pulp* is such a contrast to *Get Carter* that it seems to have been rather forgotten. Rarely seen on television, virtually never seen at the Cinematheques and unavailable on video or DVD, it is easy to see why it is a film that has made little impact. But think again. *Pulp* is funny, weird and often quite wonderful, and once again Caine offers Mike Hodges a top-rate performance. The opening scenes of Caine's pulp writer dictating his latest tacky masterpiece are to be cherished and Mickey Rooney gives one of the performances of his career as the vain but fading Hollywood star. *Pulp* is certainly an oddity - distributors did not know how to handle it - but it probably remains one of Caine's least-known films and deserves the opportunity to be seen. Catch it if you can!

5. The Terminal Man (1974)

Cast: George Segal (Harry Benson), Joan Hackett (Dr Janet Ross), Richard A Dysart (Dr John Ellis), Donald Moffat (Dr Arthur McPherson), Michael C Gwynne (Dr Robert Morris), William Hansen (Dr Ezra Manon), Jill Clayburgh (Angela Black), James Sikking (Ralph Friedman)

Crew: Director Mike Hodges, Screenplay Mike Hodges. Novel Michael Crichton, Producer Mike Hodges, Associate Producer Michael Dryhurst, Cinematographer Richard H Kline, Editor Robert L Wolfe, Art Director Fred Harpman, Costumes Donald Brooks & Vittorio Nino Novarese, Incidental Music Johann Sebastian Bach played by Glenn Gould. 99 minutes.

Story: Armed police board a helicopter. There is a discussion between doctors at a flash Los Angeles rooftop restaurant. Their serious conversation is deflected when one asks if that is Paul Newman across the way. They are discussing the case of computer programmer Harry Benson who, following an injury in a road crash, suffers from seizures which trigger bouts of vicious ultra-violence. The doctors plan to admit him to hospital for a ground-breaking experimental operation to plant electrodes in his brain and hence control his violence.

Benson is brought to the slick and sleek hospital by armed police, and placed in a guarded room. While there a girlfriend, Angela Black, brings him a bag containing many things, including a blond wig. Though the doctors have thought clearly and analytically about the operation, there are some dissenting voices, in particular, his psychiatrist Dr Janet Ross. Benson, though, has agreed to the operation, has his head shaved and, in a chilling sequence, his brain is drilled and electrodes fitted.

After the operation, Benson says he feels "like a time bomb waiting to go off," and undergoes a series of tests to check the electrodes. These send tiny electric shocks into his brain to neutralise the seizures whenever they occur. Soon after the initial session, the seizures increase in frequency. The doctors realise that

Benson's brain has become addicted to the shocks, and is triggering seizures to obtain further stimulation.

Benson escapes from the hospital and arranges to be picked up by Angela Black. The doctors speculate that Benson's next seizure will be in a few hours and, sure enough, as he and Angela enjoy a little quality time together a seizure hits him. Grabbing a pair of scissors, Benson attacks her on the waterbed, viciously stabbing both her and the bed. His next seizure sees him destroy the robots and computers at the laboratory where he used to work, and then he attacks a priest at a church.

As Dr Janet Ross, now back at home, emerges from her shower she finds Benson waiting at the bottom of the stairs. With another seizure imminent, she grabs a knife and stabs him in the chest. She flees to the bathroom, and hides in the shower as he tries to smash his way through the wall, whimpering with pain as the seizure mounts.

Benson staggers, pistol in hand, through a graveyard, weaves through the tombstones and water sprinklers before stumbling into a freshly-dug grave. As Dr Ross tries to talk with him, the police helicopter hovers above the grave and the marksman shoots him dead. The final shot is the police helicopter landing on the same pad as in the opening shot.

Background: With the serious science-fiction thriller *The Terminal Man*, Mike Hodges took another change of direction - though not necessarily a deliberate one. He said: "I'm a bit bizarre really in terms of what I seem to have ended up working on. John Calley at Warner Bros. sent me the Michael Crichton book *The Terminal Man*. It was a very serious piece and they wanted me to adapt, produce and direct it. I suppose after *Pulp* I must have wanted to do something weighty. There were no laughs in *The Terminal Man* at all. I said I would do it because the subject interested me, and, of course, I was interested in working in Hollywood - just to see what it was like. I immediately hated Los Angeles. Maybe it was because of the depression I was experiencing at the time. I'm glad to say that it passed while I was there, but initially it was awful. I was also terrified - I was producing, writing and directing out there in Hollywood for the first time!

"Having used only locations with *Get Carter* and *Pulp*, I had to be dragged kicking and screaming into the studio. There is a major operation sequence in the film that runs for over 30 minutes. Although I was desperate to shoot it in a real hospital, there was really nowhere we could do it. We looked at every conceivable operating theatre in Los Angeles, and eventually the production designer Fred Hartman convinced me that we should build our own at the studio. I am eternally grateful to him.

"I just loved filming in the studio. I adored it! For a film-maker it is bliss. It is like working in a magic box where you can do anything. You can make it rain. You can make it snow. You can make the sun shine. Sound and light are under your total control. Everything is possible."

Hodges met the book's author Michael Crichton (now established as a powerful creative force behind the likes of *Jurassic Park* and *ER*, but at that time he had not yet directed a film) before production began and recalled that Crichton had originally been slated to write and direct the film for Warner Brothers. "But I didn't know that at the time. Out of courtesy I sent him a copy of my script," said Hodges. "I had changed the ending radically. In his book there was a shoot-up in the hospital basement but I wanted somewhere more symbolic. An unoccupied grave seemed just the ticket. Practically the first place I went to see when I got to LA was Forest Hills. He wrote me a very pleasant letter, but made it clear he didn't like my new ending."

When preparing the film, Hodges originally wanted to shoot in black and white but the studio would not let him. The shape rather that the tone of the film was influenced from another source. "The American painter Edward Hopper was relatively unknown here in those days. I certainly had never heard of him. Something made me pick up a book of his paintings in Pickwick's bookshop on Hollywood Boulevard. I opened it and there was my film. There was the loneliness of urban America on every page. I can remember stripping my film down to match the loneliness that Hopper had captured."

The Terminal Man, though not released in the UK, was successful in Japan and, according to Hodges, it was dumped when it came to US screenings. "We had one terrible preview. They projected it without sound for the first 10 minutes, which was excruciating. American audiences found the film too uncompromising, too tough to take. The reviews were dire.

"I think people had a problem accepting George Segal in the lead role. At that time he was known as a light comedian, but I wanted him for the film. I liked the fact that it was unusual casting. He is terribly good in it and, now that his career is not so top heavy with comedy, you can see him purely as an actor - and a good one."

There are certain links to Hodges' television piece *The Manipulators*, and Hodges points out that the key to *The Terminal Man* is the way that the main character is manipulated. "If you want an illustration of audience manipulation just watch the scenes where they are testing the electrodes to find the pleasure cells they are going to activate. It is very Pavlovian. The subject also interested me because the hero is fearful of machines and is about their manipulation of us. I think this is a subject that has become more and more relevant.

"In the middle of this nightmare of abusive reviews, with the film being dumped, out of the blue came a fan letter from Terrence Malick, who had just made *Badlands*, also for Warner Brothers. The letter was a eulogy, the one bright light in the darkness.

"I learned one thing from this experience. As producer/director I brought the film in under budget and on schedule, but when it came to selling it, protecting it, I am hopeless. I just can't go out and hustle. So *The Terminal Man* just died. It was just too serious and uncomfortable for the distributors.

"The great thing is, though, that I still get large residuals from *The Terminal Man*. Why? Because it's screened so much on American television. It did find its audience in the end - albeit on television."

Themes/Subtext: It is easy to see why Hodges would be interested in the idea of science and surgery trying to change the behaviour of a man. Pavlovian response was a theme in Hodges' television short *The Manipulators*, and at the core of *The Terminal Man* are the serious issues of whether or not it is right to meddle with the brain and if experimentation on criminals should be advocated. Despite the fact that this was Hodges' first US-shot film, he obviously found America amusing - and Los Angeles in particular - so the doctors are more interested in spotting movie stars in the restaurant than they are in discussing the medical matters at hand. In their clinical environment, the doctors are dehumanised and the helpless Segal the only point of humanity. Hodges also pinpoints money and power as the real reason behind George Segal's surgery, not a genuine concern for his case.

The Verdict: Maybe George Segal playing a psychotic killer worried both the studio and audiences. However, he is exceptionally good and the film itself is excellently structured and quite fascinating. For modern audiences the plotting seems a little slow at times, e.g. the central brain surgery scene seems to drag on, but it is a stunning contrast to films at the time, in that it offers paranoia and subtle thrills rather than out-and-out action. Important issues are raised, but it also has some old-fashioned chills and thrills. In many ways this is also a modern-day Frankenstein's monster at loose in a trendy 1970s Los Angeles, with the atmosphere much enhanced by pianist Glenn Gould's eerie music. Again, something of a lost film that could well stand some re-evaluation.

6. Interlude I: Screenplays And Near Misses

Mid-Atlantic (1975) [unproduced]

When he was in Hollywood making *The Terminal Man*, Mike Hodges was given a book called *The Pit* to read. It was about a company called Holiday Magic who would sell cosmetics to their sellers at a big discount so that the products could be sold on at a profit. When the products hadn't shifted, the company would suggest the sellers take part in a course on leadership dynamics.

"They would then convince these people to cough up $1,000 to go for a weekend leadership course. It was before all of those fashionable mind-expanding courses started up. The book was about one of these courses going wrong, turning violent. It described how, when you walked into the room for the course, you were confronted by a coffin, a crucifix, a hangman's rope and a full-size cage, all to be used for psychological inspiration. The book seemed to examine in a dramatic way everything that concerned me.

"I gave it to this Warner Brothers executive and said I would recreate it with actors over two weekends for free. He read it and was absolutely horrified. Or was it that all of the excesses of the capitalist system were laid bare? It was about greed and the perversion of everything! It showed all of the worst elements of American life!

"Back in the UK a friend told me that the same course had come here in 1975. I researched what had happened when a reporter had infiltrated the course, and blew the operation apart. The course operators just vanished. I decided to write a black comedy called *Mid-Atlantic*. In it, a seedy PR man in a seaside resort here, out of season, who had always wanted to escape to America, gets a call asking if he can negotiate a deal with a hotel to accommodate a special course that was coming to town."

Hodges wrote the script and had actor Malcolm McDowell lined up to play the PR man, but then spent four years trying to get the project funded. "I passionately believed in this piece. It was a wicked satire on capitalism. I had one scene with a man hanging from the cross being questioned about selling life insurance. But I can't hustle. I just couldn't get it made. I would get certain elements together and then something else would fall through."

In that four-year period trying to get *Mid-Atlantic* off the ground, Hodges also wrote two other scripts (*The Chilean Club* (1976) and *Spare Parts* (1977)), neither of which attracted any backing. "By 1974 I'd had a pretty good innings. I had made three interesting films, but now in 1978 I had also had four years out. I had only made three films in seven years, so I thought I had better make another one."

Damien: Omen II (1978)

Cast: William Holden (Richard Thorn), Lee Grant (Ann Thorn), Jonathan Scott-Taylor (Damien), Robert Foxworth (Paul Buher), Nicholas Pryor (Charles Warren), Lew Ayres (Bill Atherton), Sylvia Sidney (Aunt Marion), Lance Henriksen (Sergeant Neff).

Crew: Director Don Taylor (Mike Hodges directed for three weeks), Writers Stanley Mann & Mike Hodges (story by Harvey Bernhard). 107 minutes.

Story: Damien Thorn reads *The Book Of Revelations* and discovers all about his true past. Now that he has got rid of his parents (played by Gregory Peck and Lee Remick in *The Omen* (1976)). he is looked after by his uncle, a business executive played by William Holden. The film is set seven years after the original film, with Damien now aged 12 and set to attend a very fancy military academy.

In a similar style to *The Omen*, whenever people start to harbour dark suspicions that Damien may not be exactly as he seems, nasty things tend to happen to them. In this version, freakish deaths include one chap getting squashed between railroad cars, another being attacked by a raven and a third dying under the ice of a frozen river. In this film the emphasis is not on others suspecting the truth about Damien, but Damien coming to terms with what he is.

At times he is confused and upset about the awful truth, but he gets used to it. Zealots who know and relish the fact that he is the Antichrist, do all they can to help him along his evil path.

Damien proves rather adept in his Antichrist duties, and manages to excel at the extremely autocratic military school. Then he makes sure that he will eventually take over his uncle's multinational company Thorn Corporation. Roll on *Omen III*.

Background: "They had originally asked me to make *The Omen* but I found the script absolutely laughable. I must say that in the end the director Richard Donner did an absolutely brilliant job with unpromising material.

"Then I was offered the sequel, which was far more interesting because the subject was highly political. The corporation owned by Damien's uncle was cornering the world's food markets and introducing genetically modified food. It also featured scenes in an American military school which, having been to Vietnam, fascinated me. They are such terrifying places and I was interested in exploring the brutalisation of the American male. So I thought this synopsis was great! It was unwittingly anti-capitalist and here I was being offered it by an American conglomerate, 20th Century-Fox . Very amusing. So I said yes!"

Hodges worked on the script and filming began in Chicago but, after three weeks, by mutual agreement , he left the project. "If you look at the film you can clearly see the bits that I shot [Hodges filmed the scenes in the military academy and the food laboratories], but after those three weeks it was such a nightmare that I was glad to get out. I had a meeting with the Fox people, who said I was shooting too slow, but I don't think that was the real reason. I said I was happy to leave the film, and that I would carry on until such time as they had an alternative director. They didn't tell me that they had already found someone to replace me!

"I think essentially I was uncomfortable with the film and the Fox people probably recognised that. I was making a political film whereas they were making a horror film. It became apparent that I was not going to produce the goods from their point of view. They had a highly commercial franchise and I think I knew in my heart of hearts that I wouldn't be able to deliver what they wanted.

"What they wanted was the antithesis of everything I stood for in film-making. There were many interesting things in the story, which was why I took it on, but that's not enough. In the end it was my fault."

After he left *Damien: Omen II*, Hodges wrote two original scripts which were never filmed (*Blood And Thunder* (1970) and *Say Goodnight, Lilian - Goodnight* (1978)) but admits that he also began to wonder if his film-making career might be over. Then, out of the blue, came a telephone call from his friend the director Nic Roeg, which would lead on to his involvement with the cult/camp science-fiction classic *Flash Gordon*.

7. Flash! Ah ah...

Flash Gordon (1980)

Cast: Sam J Jones (Flash Gordon), Melody Anderson (Dale Arden), Max Von Sydow (The Emperor Ming), Topol (Dr Hans Zharkov), Ornella Muti (Princess Aura), Timothy Dalton (Prince Barin), Brian Blessed (Prince Vultan), Peter Wyngarde (Klytus), Mariangela Melato (Kala), John Osborne (Arborian Priest), Richard O'Brien (Fico).

Crew: Director Mike Hodges, Screenwriter Lorenzo Semple Jr., Adaptation Michael Allin, Comic Strips Alex Raymond, Producer Dino De Laurentiis, Executive Producer Bernard Williams, Cinematographer Gilbert Taylor, Editor Malcolm Cooke, Production Designer Danilo Donati, Art Director John Graysmark, Music Queen and Howard Blake. 111 minutes.

Story: The planet Earth is being hit by meteor showers, storms and tornadoes - it is the evil Emperor Ming playing with the planet before its planned annihilation. Cue the memorable 'Flash Gordon' theme song from Queen, and an impressive credits sequence using moving cut-outs from Alex Raymond's original *Flash Gordon* strip cartoon.

At a small airport American Football star Flash Gordon is waiting for his plane to arrive. He gets on board with the attractive Dale Arden, who he had seen the night before at the Dark Harbour Inn. As the plane takes off, flaming hail starts to fall - the evil laugh of Ming can be heard in the distance. Meanwhile, the terrible weather conditions confirm the worst suspicions of scientist Dr Zharkov, a former NASA man who was sacked because he voiced his suspicions that the planet was being attacked from outer space. He plans to launch his own rocket - which he built in his greenhouse - to go and tackle the enemy, but his assistant is not keen on joining him on the flight.

The pilots are sucked out of Flash's plane and it crash-lands into Zharkov's greenhouse. The batty scientist lures Flash and Dale into the rocket and, after a short tussle, the launch button is pressed and they fly off into space, eventually landing on the Planet Mongo, close to Ming's palace. The threesome are captured and taken to Ming's court where they witness the squabbling between the Hawkman Prince Vultan and the Arborian Prince Barin, as well as the innate cruelty of the Emperor Ming.

The hunky Flash is observed by Ming's sultry daughter Princess Aura (who has a pet human named Fellini', making Dale a little jealous. However, when Ming announces he plans to take Dale for his 'pleasure,' Flash gets upset and battles the guards using his American Football skills (he throws metal football-shaped objects at them), before being knocked out because of a bad pass by Zharkov.

Flash is to be executed, but his death is faked by the eager Princess Aura and he is spirited away. Meanwhile Zharkov is brainwashed by Ming's right-hand man Klytus, and Dale is prepared for Ming's pleasure. Aura shows Flash how to communicate by telepathy and he 'calls' Dale to tell her all is well. She escapes and teams up with Zharkov, who, it turns out, hadn't been brainwashed at all due to his prodigious brainpower and ability to remember Beatles' songs.

Aura takes Flash to Arboria. Her lover Prince Barin is not pleased to see her arrive with another man in tow, so when Aura returns to Mongo he plots to kill Flash. Zharkov and Dale are captured by Hawkmen and are taken to Prince Vultan's floating city, where they try and convince the jolly leader of the Hawkmen that Flash will lead them in a revolt against Ming.

Barin and Flash are also captured and taken to Prince Vultan. Barin insists he fight Flash to the death, and they duel on a floating platform replete with retractable spikes. Dale shouts out, "Flash! I love you! But we only have 14 hours to save the Earth!" Ming and his robotic hordes arrive and, after Flash turns down the chance to rule a partially-destroyed Earth, Ming takes away Zharkov, Dale and Barin. As Ming bombards the floating palace, Flash jumps onto a rocket cycle and flies off to join Vultan and his band of Hawkmen.

Flash and the Hawkmen capture Ming's war rocket Ajax and attack the palace as Ming and Dale prepare to wed. Barin and Zharkov are freed by Princess Aura (she has a change of heart after being tortured by Klytus), and they turn off the palace's defences. Flash flies the war rocket right into the palace and, with exceptional aim, he impales Ming on the sharpened point of the rocket ship.

All is well...Earth is saved and all can live happily ever after!

Background: "Out of the blue I had a call from Nic Roeg. We'd been friends for a while and he called me up and said Dino De Laurentiis wanted to meet me. So I went to a meeting at the Connaught Hotel and met up with Nic and the writer Michael Allin, who were doing *Flash Gordon* at the time, in Dino's suite.

"Then Dino took me into the bedroom and asked me if I wanted to make the sequel. I said I didn't know anything about Flash Gordon, but Dino insisted I read the script. He wanted to make use of the sets once they had been built. I don't know if Nic suggested me or what, but I took Michael Allin's script away and read it and thought about it. I didn't know anything about special effects and decided I wasn't the right person for the job and so I said 'No.' Soon afterwards, unbeknown to me, Nic's production designer had fallen out with Dino and the whole thing had unravelled and they all ended up parting company.

"One lunchtime I was in a restaurant in Soho, nobody knew where I was, not even my wife, and the maître d' came up and said I was wanted on the phone. It was Bernie Williams, who was Dino's line producer. He said Dino wanted me to fly to New York to talk about directing the film. How he found me I never knew but it shows how persistent he is."

Hodges conferred with his two sons, who were keen he should make the film, so he agreed to meet with Dino. "I got on Concorde for the first time with all of the businessmen. They opened their briefcases and took out their computer read-outs while I took out my bumper volume of Flash Gordon! It must have been an odd sight. They probably thought I was retarded. Anyway I went through all of the comics during the flight. At the end of it I still thought to myself that I shouldn't do it.

"I met with Dino and Danilo Donati, his new production designer. Danilo had done a lot of Federico Fellini films - including one of my favourites, *Casanova* - great, but he spoke no English at all! He had completed drawings that must have been about eight feet high by twenty feet long, which his assistants unravelled to show to me. These were crazy enormous sets of Arboria and Mongo - I'd never seen anything so insane! What made me take it on? Basically Dino talked me into doing it.

"Also I needed a film to salvage my career!" Hodges worked on the script with Lorenzo Semple Jr. and then started shooting some of the model work. "That's when Dino and I had our one and only bust-up. He had looked at rushes without telling me, which is unpardonable. I was already awed by the task ahead of me so perhaps I used this as an excuse to resign. Talking with Dino on the phone - for weeks he called me Nic by mistake - was bizarre because he was already calling to an assistant for his list of directors. I'm told that when I hung up he pointed at a name and said 'get him.' The name he pointed at was 'Mike Hodges.' I'm not sure he knew who I was, or that he'd ever employed me. Eventually we made up, talked the problems through, and I stumbled back to the film."

At the early pre-production stage, Kurt Russell did a camera test for the part of Flash Gordon, and Dennis Hopper was among the names considered for Zharkov. It was Dino's mother-in-law, though, who spotted Sam J Jones on a US TV show titled *Hollywood Squares* and she suggested him for the lead role. As Jones commented in *Film Review*: "That's right. Dino's mother-in-law saw me and called Dino, and then Dino called me for an interview. I was working for Blake Edwards on *10* in Hawaii with Dudley Moore at the time and I got this call to fly to LA to meet with Dino De Laurentiis. This was in 1978 for the first interview. Evidently, from what I was told afterwards, he looked at a lot of different prospects." In 1979 Jones flew to London for a screen test, and four weeks later got the message that he was Flash. His hair was dyed blond, and special blue contact lenses were made for him, though eventually he didn't use them in the movie because they were an irritant.

Next was the casting of Flash's would-be girlfriend Dale Arden. As Mike Hodges recalled in *Film Review*: "We did several camera tests and cast this Canadian actress as Dale. Then Dino decided she was too thin, that the poor woman didn't have enough fun about her. We'd already auditioned Melody Anderson and done a camera test, so we just switched to her, and I thought she was wonderful in the film."

Commenting about the 10-month production period, he added: "Truthfully, it always felt out of control, and the only way I could cope was to relax, let go. I normally keep a tight control on my films - but with this one I just had to let go. Basically, I just improvised everything. Danilo Donati built the sets pretty much for himself, same with the costumes, which he also designed. The practicalities of film-making never bothered him. I'm not sure he ever read the script. Each day I would simply wait to see what I was presented with and improvise. Once I got the hang of it, it was great. For example when it was time for the Pig Men to come on set they couldn't find it because they had no way of seeing out of their costumes. So I made them blind. Perfect. In another scene Dale is meant to knock out the same Pig Men with karate kicks and chops. When Melody Anderson came on set she was clad in a heavy metal dress with high-heeled shoes! She could hardly walk let alone perform karate. So I had her take the shoes off and leave them on the floor like they were outside a hotel room waiting to be cleaned. From there we built up a dance-cum-fight routine in which she would move the shoes along with each bit of action.

"I was lucky with *Flash Gordon* because I was shooting in the UK with a great crew, a loyal crew, and so I was able to relax and make it up as I went along. I think it was this that gave the film such a light touch, a soufflé effect, and maybe that is why it works. It was always exuberant, alive, not dead, even while we were making it. We went back to Alex Raymond's original strip cartoons, full of exotic primary colours, and the great thing was that it appealed to adults and children alike.

According to Mike Hodges, the cast as well as the crew enjoyed the experience of largely improvising the film. "The thrust of each scene remained, but we often changed the dialogue and I would add lines. The extraordinary thing was that Dino didn't realise that *Flash Gordon* was a comedy. He seriously thought we were making a science fiction action film. We would go to rushes each morning and the crew would roar with laughter. Dino couldn't understand and would ask what they were laughing about. In the end I had to ban all laughs during the rushes.

"I'm not sure how Dino thought we could do it as a serious film. Since the original strip men had gone to the moon and we had Dr Zharkov building a space rocket in his greenhouse! It had to be a comedy! It was terrific fun - tremendously exhilarating with actors like Max, Brian Blessed, Peter Wyngarde, Topol on set - but the great thing about Dino was that he had access to actors such as Max and Ornella Muti and Mariangela Melato, who were quite wonderful."

Hodges also managed to recruit playwright John Osborne, who had so memorably played Kinnear in *Get Carter*. Osborne has just a couple of scenes midway through the film, playing the Arborian priest who is in charge of the ancient ritual of manhood that sees young Arborian warriors plunge their arms into an ancient tree stump hoping they don't get stung by a nasty wood beast. The film was also made at a time when film and computer technology were in the early stages of getting together. Added Hodges in *Film Review*: "The effects were incredibly primitive in those days compared to what we have now. We had no computer imagery whatsoever. It was all done against blue backgrounds and then superimposed. The Hawkmen were done that way - layer upon layer of them. The problem then was to make sure it looked moderately real, although in a way with a film like *Flash*, it wasn't absolutely essential, because it wasn't a realistic film to begin with."

There were also problems in the post-production period, with sections of Sam J Jones' dialogue post-synched by another actor. Said Jones in *Film Review*: "I went home for Christmas and then got busy doing another project. I was supposed to go back after Christmas to do the looping and the dubbing, but it never happened. He (Hodges) got another actor in to try and match my voice, which hurt a great deal. I never had a Richard Burton-type speaking voice, but the actor he hired had this extremely high voice." Jones claims that Flash in the film is 20% his voice and 80% the other actor, adding it was "very humiliating," though Hodges says that Flash is "mostly his voice," adding that it was Jones' agent who would not let the actor return to the UK for looping. He added: "You are walking a tightrope with a film like *Flash Gordon*. Whilst it is funny, it also has to be an action film for kids. It switches when necessary and still works. For instance, when Flash has only minutes to save the earth it has to become pure Saturday morning cinema."

Themes/Subtext: This is classic Saturday morning entertainment. Producer Dino De Laurentiis may have thought he was getting action adventure, but Mike Hodges knew he was playing it for laughs. Very much a case of creating a story to fit in with the production design and the costumes, Hodges still managed to touch on a few familiar bases. Once again the Pavlovian themes shine through, especially in the sequences of Zharkov being supposedly brainwashed and then controlled by the evil Klytus. Flash Gordon may be no Jack Carter, but once again he is a hero in an - extremely - alien environment. This time, though, he is a hero who unites the forces around him rather than bumping them off. This is also the first Hodges film that manages to find room for strong female characters (they are hardly evident in *Get Carter*, *Pulp* or *The Terminal Man*), though clearly there is more fun to be had with the evil seductress Princess Aura (played by Italian actress Ornella Muti) than with the rather bland Dale. Hodges also uses the film to pay tribute to his cinematic hero Federico Fellini. The fact that Fellini regular Danilo Donati was behind much of the production style enabled Hodges to give the film a real chic Fellini feel, though how the Italian master reacted to having Muti drag around at the end of a leash a heavily made-up actor of restricted growth called Fellini is not known.

The Verdict: Described by the revered American film critic Pauline Kael as 'disco in the sky,' *Flash Gordon* is brash, funny, colourful and made with tongue firmly in cheek. When *Flash Gordon* was released it was a perfect antidote to the seriousness of sci-fi epics like *Star Wars*. The film veers from cheerfully camp to amusingly stylish, and certainly there can be no doubt that Max Von Sydow makes the perfect Ming the Merciless and Ornella Muti the most seductive Princess Aura. In-jokes and knowing sexiness for the adults and action and comedy for the kids, *Flash Gordon* has it all. The special effects may appear clunky, but somehow they suit the style and mood of the film, bringing it closer to the sexy camp qualities of the soft porn rip-off *Flesh Gordon* than to the sleek pyrotechnics of *Star Wars*. Plus, the music from rock band Queen works quite perfectly on the soundtrack.

8. Interlude II: Fellini And A Return To Television

Missing Pieces (1983)

Cast: Elizabeth Montgomery (Sara Scott), Ron Karabatsos (Claude Papazian), John Reilly (Sam), Louanne (Valerie Scott), Robin Gammell (Lawrence Conrad), Julius Harris (Spencer Harris), David Haskell (Andy Scott), Daniel Pilon (Jorge Mantinez).

Crew: Director Mike Hodges, Writer Mike Hodges, Novel *A Private Investigation* Karl Alexander, Cinematographer Charles Correll, Producer Doug Chapin, Editor Jim Oliver, Production Designer Fred Harpman, Costumes Francis Hayes & Brad R Loman. CBS. Transmission date: May 14, 1983. 96 minutes.

Story: Television star Elizabeth Montgomery (she made her name as the star of the fantasy series *Bewitched*) stars as Sara Scott, a widow-turned-private investigator, who is constantly haunted by the murder of her journalist husband eight years ago. She takes on a case, with the assistance of cynical private eye Claude Papazian, which eventually leads her to the truth behind her husband's death.

Background: Originally titled *A Private Investigation*, *Missing Pieces* was a made-for-television thriller shot in 1982, but first screened in 1983. "I was getting divorced at this point and I thought it was probably best if I got out of the country. It was just so painful. So I was offered this book by CBS to adapt for Elizabeth Montgomery. It was interesting in many ways - I liked the book and the arena where it takes place - but for me it was a job that kept me busy and away from the UK for a while."

And The Ship Sails On (E La Nave Va) (1983)

Cast: Freddie Jones (Orlando), Barbara Jefford (Ildebranda Cuffari), Victor Poletti (Aureliano Fuciletto), Peter Cellier (Sir Reginald J Dongby), Elisa Mainardi (Teressa Valegnani), Norma West (Lady Violet Dongby Albertini), Pablo Paolini (Il Maestro Albertini).

Crew: Director Federico Fellini, Screenwriters Catherine Breillat & Tonino Guerva, Cinematographer Giuseppe Rotunno, Production Designer Dante Ferretti, Editor Ruggero Mastroianni, Costumes Maurizio Millenotti, Music Gianfranco Plenizio, English language dubbing direction Mike Hodges. 132 minutes.

Story: It is 1914. While the world waits for the arrival of World War I, a handful of opera stars, their families and various other hangers-on set off on a funeral voyage on a chartered cruise ship carrying with them the ashes of a recently-deceased and much-revered opera diva who is to be buried in the land of her birth. The sudden arrival, however, of a group of Balkan refugees exposes the aristocratic decadence of the opera lovers as the various types of human cargo are forced to confront each other. Fellini wanted the film to show the excesses of the aristocratic classes, who were to be snuffed out by the Great War. The film contains various magical Fellini touches, including a rhinoceros being lifted from the ship's hold and the starving refugee children straining at the windows of the first-class dining room as the upper-class diners complain about their presence.

Background: In 1983 Mike Hodges had the opportunity to work - in a rather tangential way - with one his cinema heroes, the acclaimed Italian director Federico Fellini. Hodges directed the dubbing of the English language version of *And The Ship Sails On*, though his involvement in the project came from a rather unusual source.

"What happened was that Fellini rang up Stanley Kubrick and said he always had a terrible time dubbing his films into English. The results never pleased him. Stanley recommended that he get a name director to do the dubbing. That's what he did in each country where his films were released. That way the film will be treated with a director's sensibility. It seems that Stanley had always loved my work - I'd heard this from Malcolm McDowell - and so he suggested my name.

"I had major surgery at the beginning of 1983 and was in quite bad shape. That's when I had this call from Fellini and went out to Rome to meet him and see the film. I loved it. I came back here and, since most of the actors in it were English, the work wasn't too hard. They had a guide track, albeit a bad one. It was so interesting watching each scene time and time again - seeing how Fellini worked. I learnt so much and it was a great job to get because I was quite frail. At least I could work sitting down.

"I worked with Danilo Donati on *Flash* for almost a year, during which my admiration of his talent and inventiveness grew and grew. The theatricality of his work with Fellini obviously interested me, and I winkled out of him how they created so many amazing visual effects. When it came to working on *Squaring The Circle*, I put a lot of what I had picked up from him to good effect."

Squaring The Circle (1984)

Cast: Bernard Hill (Lech Walesa), Alec McGowen (Rakowski), Roy Kinnear (Kania), John Woodvine (Gierek), Richard Kane (Jaruzelski), Don Henderson (Kuron), Frank Middlemass (Brezhnev), John Bluthal (Babiuch), Richard Crenna (The Narrator).

Crew: Director Mike Hodges, Screenwriter Tom Stoppard, Producer Frederick Brogger, Executive Producers Peter Snell & Stephen Schlow, Cinematographer Michael Garfath, Production Designer Voytek, Editors John Bloom & Eric Boyd-Perkins, Music Roy Budd. A TVS production in association with Metromedia Production Corporation with Britannic Film & Television. 110 minutes.

Story: *Squaring The Circle* is about the Polish Solidarity movement and its charismatic leader Lech Walesa. A deliberately studio-set television production, the story is narrated by Richard Crenna who takes an often ironic look at the development of Solidarity and the internal workings of the Polish political and social systems. At the start, the Polish politicians are clearly still in the thrall of their Soviet bosses but in the shipyards of Gdansk there is a little strike brewing and a certain Lech Walesa (who doesn't appear until halfway into the production) is drawing substantial support.

Initially, the Polish authorities, wary of the impact workers' strikes can have on the country, go through the motions of visibly supporting the Solidarity movement but it is still the Soviet authorities who are pulling the strings. Much is made of the legal registration of the Solidarity movement, though the authorities try to stipulate that Solidarity acknowledges the leading role of the Party in the running of Poland.

While the power and popularity of Solidarity grows, so does the profile of Walesa, who even visits Rome to meet with the Pope. Solidarity enters into further disputes with the ruling Government over the five-day week and, under the glare of the media (and further changes in the ruling party led by Brezhnev and the Soviets) an agreement is finally reached. In a final irony, Walesa signs the agreement using a Mickey Mouse pen.

Background: "I was about the eighth director to be asked to crack it - I know Alan Clarke and John Irvin were approached. Stoppard's script wasn't very filmic. But I suppose my recent exposure to Donati and Fellini influenced me. I knew how to do it! The thing about Stoppard is his sheer enjoyment of words - wonderful witty speeches that encapsulate the human comedy, which I knew would be best presented in a studio where the actors would be able to deliver them in comfort, without any interruptions from the outside world, like aircraft and cars.

"My production designer was Voytek, an old Polish friend of mine, though we had never worked together before. Over one weekend we came up with a design kit that would enable us to accommodate the enormous number of different locations Tom had in his script. We would build a great metal rig with gantries and steps, a basic set that we could adapt with simple props - a bust of Lenin, corrugated iron, a bookcase, red curtains - for every scene in Tom's script.

"I was still recovering from surgery and was very weak. Needless to say I couldn't tell anybody or I wouldn't have got the job. This was one film I *had* to make. I knew I was right for it. It was hard to do such a complicated piece in just 24 days.

"There was a sequence of key scenes placed throughout the film, which involved Brezhnev meeting the succession of Polish leaders at a beach on the Black Sea. TVS, my employer, agreed that I could shoot in the studio, but with the proviso that I shot the beach scenes on location. Although I knew that the intrusion of a real location would destroy the conceit of the whole piece I sort of agreed, playing for time.

"When I neared the end of the shoot the producers said they couldn't afford the cost of going on location. That's when my conversations with Danilo paid off. I knew exactly how to create the illusion of a beach in the studio. I had Voytek get several truckloads of pebbles to the set, then run a vast sheet of clear plastic away from the pebbles up to the studio cyclorama. We next pumped a lot of light so that it kicked off the plastic, like the sun does off the sea, and finally added a wind machine to give it movement. Hey presto, we had a marvellous beach which also retained the sense of suspend reality that ran through the film."

As enjoyable as making *Squaring The Circle* had been, it was somewhat soured when Hodges discovered that the US co-producer wanted to re-edit the film and then came upon composer Roy Budd recording music for an American version he hadn't been told about. He didn't mince his words when confronting the producers and Tom Stoppard.

"*Squaring The Circle* was also shown at the Banff Television Festival, where it was awarded the Critics' Prize, a Rocky, but more importantly a cheque for $10,000. I would never have known any of this if Gus McDonald (who had worked with Hodges in his early days in television) hadn't been there. He sent a card congratulating me. I was in Vancouver a week later and rang the festival organisers, asking what had happened to my prize. They told me the money was to be split between the production designer and the cameraman. The producers had tried to cut me out altogether. If I hadn't made that call I'd never have seen a cent. And I never ever saw the Rocky."

9. From Outer Space To The Florida Straits

Morons From Outer Space (1985)

Cast: Mel Smith (Bernard), Griff Rhys Jones (Graham Sweetley), James Sikking (Colonel Laribee), Sean Barry-Weste (Doomsday Man), Jimmy Nail (Desmond Brock), Paul Bown (Julian Tope), Joanne Pearce (Sandra Brock), Dinsdale Landen (Commander Matteson).

Crew: Director Mike Hodges, Screenwriters Mel Smith & Griff Rhys Jones, Producer Barry Hanson, Cinematographer Phil Meheux, Editor Peter Boyle, Production Designers Bert Davey & Brian Eatwell, Music Peter Brewis. 97 minutes.

Story: Aimed fairly and squarely as an antidote to the antiseptic notions of cuddly and clever aliens, *Morons From Outer Space* sadly feels often like an extended television pilot rather than a fully-fledged feature film. The film opens somewhere in outer space, where a spacecraft stops at an intergalactic petrol station to refuel. Unfortunately, while the Captain is sorting out the refuelling process, one of his dumber-than-dumb companions starts playing with the controls, accidentally starts the engines and manages to send the craft on a collision course with the planet Earth. They happen to land in the middle of a motorway.

The landing of these extraterrestrials causes something of a sensation on earth, but rather than a close encounter with a sophisticated and intelligent species as the Earthbound authorities are expecting, it turns out that these ETs are stupider than the average human, and have a worse sense of dress to boot. No *Star Trek*-type bridge for them. Forget computer screens, flashing buttons and sleek buffed metal. The moronic aliens have a cockpit looking like a pinewood kitchen. These are really just trailer-trash space folk who happened to have taken a wrong turn.

The more the military interrogate them to try and find out space-age secrets and the mysteries of the universe, the more they are hit with the fact that these are just aliens who are plain dumb. It turns out that the foursome are from the planet Blob and were simply taking a bit of a holiday. Despite the fact that some of the generals still believe that the ETs are simply faking the whole thing, three of the morons find themselves on the chat show circuit, while one (Bernard) is actually mistaken for a human and put right into a mental institution. Bernard manages to escape and gathers up his buddies for a final rendezvous with their mothership.

Background: Mike Hodges was approached by an old friend, the producer Verity Lambert, who was head of production at EMI. She sent him *Illegal Aliens*, a script written by Mel Smith and Griff Rhys Jones who, at that time, were household names through the television show *Not The Nine O'clock News* (which also featured Rowan Atkinson and Pamela Stephenson).

"I was trying to find a base in the UK, a studio with whom I could work consistently, so I said I would be interested if EMI would back *Mid-Atlantic*, the script I had written back in 1975. Verity liked it very much, so we did a two-picture deal.

"I did *Morons From Outer Space*, which incidentally was slated by the critics here. I truly think quite unfairly. I wish Mel Smith and Griff Rhys Jones had had more time to work on the script. I kept begging them to take it more seriously because I did think it was a brilliant idea. I'm anti-Spielbergian and anti his saccharine, sentimental take on the world. I liked the idea of directing the antidote.

"Sadly there was also a falling-out in the middle of the shoot when Mel and Griff were shown a cut of the material we had shot so far. They thought my approach was too subtle, not broad enough and that I didn't understand comedy. That I don't think is true, because there's a great deal of comedy in *Get Carter* and *Pulp*. Verity also thought the lighting was too moody, not bright enough.

"For other reasons the producer and production designer were removed. In short there was major upheaval right in the middle of the shoot. So instead of the script problems being corrected I ended up letting the actors go over the top and putting more light on them. Both were against my grain. In retrospect I think if it had been played more realistically it would have been better. That said, it is still an okay film, and I think the first half is actually very good.

"The critics here were hateful, although it did garner my favourite review of all time: 'Die before you see this film.' I think there was a lot of cultural snobbery involved. In America it got some excellent reviews. I think Mel and Griff were shaken by the vehemence of the critical response, while I was used to it.

"Then to cap it all, Verity left her job with EMI. So I didn't get to make *Mid-Atlantic*, and my dream of having a British work base didn't materialise."

With a wry smile, Mike Hodges admits that the 1980s were not great years for him. After *Morons From Outer Space* he wrote the stage play *Soft Shoe Shuffle*, which was performed at the Lyric Hammersmith starring Frances Tomelty, and then went to work on two American productions. He also wrote an unmade screenplay called *A Cuckoo's Child* (1986).

Themes/Subtext: Though on the surface *Morons From Outer Space* may appear to be good old-fashioned comedy, Hodges in fact was also working hard at poking holes into the whole science-fiction movie genre (the aliens are initially serenaded by scientists with a five-note imitation of the *Close Encounters* theme, the music from *Born Free* and a Scott Joplin rag), while also dealing with familiar elements of characters out of place in their environments. One could say that, like Michael Caine in *Get Carter* and *Pulp*, the 'Morons' are characters doing their inept best to deal with being put into an unfamiliar environment. As Hodges notes, he is anti-Spielbergian and enjoyed deflating films such as *E.T.* and *Close Encounters Of The Third Kind*. While he was concerned that the script spent too much time lambasting the intelligence organisations, the radical socialist in him enjoyed poking fun at supposedly intelligent secret services.

The Verdict: *Morons From Outer Space* must have sounded a brilliant idea on paper (or perhaps when pitched by screenwriters/ stars Mel Smith and Griff Rhys Jones) but, in reality, while there are moments to savour, as a whole the film just doesn't work.

The Hitchhiker: WGOD (1985)

Cast: Gary Busey (Rev. Nolan Powers), Geraldine Page (Lynette), Page Fletcher (The Hitchhiker), Robert Ito (Seto), Brioni Farrell (Darlene), Gerald (Tony Lewis).

Crew: Director Mike Hodges (credited as Michael Hodges), Executive Producer Jeremy Lipp, Story Richard Rothstein, Teleplay Tom Baum, Cinematographer Thomas Burstyn, Production Designer Richard Wilcox, Editor George Appleby, Music Michel Rubibi. HBO. Transmission date: November 26, 1985. 30 minutes.

Story: The Reverend Nolan Powers hosts - and runs - the radio station WGOD ("The airwaves belong to God on 1350 AM") claiming that "confession is good for the soul" and that God is listening at all times and will sort out all problems if only the eager listeners will believe. While hosting one slot, Powers gets a mysterious call from a young man who says that Nolan is "afraid of the truth." When asked what his favourite song if the voice says it is 'What a Friend You Have in Jesus.' When Powers returns home to his palatial mansion (he drives there in a stylish Lincoln complete with a cross on the front of the bonnet), he finds his mother upstairs in the attic room listening to a recording his young brother Gerald made of 'What A Friend You Have In Jesus.'

Powers' slightly crazed mother tells him that though he is a fine son, his brother Gerald (who vanished some time ago) was perfect. On the programme the next day the mysterious voice again takes over the programme. Powers finds himself increasingly obsessed with the voice and in the driving rain rushes to his garage, takes hold of a spade and heads off in his car. The voice again talks to him via the car radio He drives to a place near to the WGOD radio station and starts digging, but the voice eventually drives him to the radio studio. There, while the station transmits his comments live on air, he admits to killing his brother out of jealousy for his mother's love. As the police finally dig up the body, the Hitchhiker is seen in the distance adding his final thoughts to the story.

Background: *The Hitchhiker* mystery thriller series ran on US television from November 1983 to February 1991, covering six seasons and featuring 85 episodes in total. Directors featured on the series included Paul Verhoeven, Phillip Noyce, Roger Vadim and Mai Zetterling. Guest stars featured over the run included Willem Dafoe, Kirstie Alley, Tom Skerritt, Klaus Kinski, Sandra Bernhard, Helen Hunt (in one of her first television roles) and Hodges' *Flash Gordon* star Ornella Muti. The episodes, all of which ran 30 minutes, were linked by the mysterious character of The Hitchhiker and were made in the style of the classic *The Twilight Zone* or *Alfred Hitchcock Presents* television mysteries. Sometimes they featured the supernatural, but more often they explored the darker twists of human nature. Nicholas Campbell played The Hitchhiker for the first season and Page Fletcher replaced him thereafter.

Mike Hodges' programme *WGOD* was episode four of the third season. It was filmed in Vancouver, Canada, and Mike Hodges has relatively fond memories of the production. He said: "I love making short films. It's like a sculptor's maquette, I often prefer them to the finished work. The short I made with Gary Busey and Geraldine Page was an interesting experience. They offered you a choice of scripts. I'm not fond of American fundamentalist preachers so I chose to do *WGOD*. But even here something went wrong. I designed this special soundtrack for the end of the film, I brought it with me from the UK. The producers were very enthusiastic when I showed them the cut film. With the soundtrack in place. I left for home. Some months later I saw it transmitted on television. They had removed the soundtrack without telling me. Why I will never know."

Florida Straits (1986)

Cast: Raul Julia (Carlos Jayne), Fred Ward (Lucky Boone), Daniel Jenkins (Mac), Jaime Sanchez (Innocente), Victor Argo (Pablo), Ilka Tanya Payan (Carmen), Antonio Fargas (El Gato Negro), Jesse Corti (Guido).

Crew: Director Mike Hodges, Producer Stuart R Rekant, Executive Producer Robert M Cooper, Screenwriter Roderick Taylor, Cinematographer Denis Lewiston, Production Designer Voytek, Art Director Mack Pittman, Costumes Moss Mabry. 97 minutes.

Story: An unsmiling Carlos Jayne arrives amongst a group of Cuban refugees at a military airport in Miami. He checks into a hotel with his few belongings, including a battered copy of Cervantes' *Don Quixote.* Soon there is a knock at the door. Carlos is attacked but manages to fight off his would-be assailant and questions him about Carmen, the woman he has left behind in Cuba. Meanwhile, boat owner Lucky Boone gambles virtually all he has on a hand of cards and loses half of his boat, the White Witch, to a gangly youth named Mac.

The next day Mac turns up at the boat and takes a share in Lucky's boat hire business. Carlos offers them work. They turn him down initially, but after a meeting in his hotel room he offers them a "broader proposition" - he wants to sneak back into Cuba and pick up $2 million in gold he hid 20 years ago, before he was sent to prison.

The boat is renamed Bruja Blanca (Spanish for White Witch), and the threesome sail to Cuba. They steal gasoline from a naval station under cover of fog, pass a heavily-mined beach area and use a small rowboat to travel inland. Carlos once worked for the CIA, while Lucky is ex-military. They make their way to a massive abandoned power station, described as "the ruins of an ancient empire - initially funded by the Batista government, but abandoned when Castro took power." They run into a band of rebels, headed by the evil El Gato Negro. They manage to escape, and Carlos leads them further into the heart of Cuba pursued by El Gato Negro.

Carlos dresses in a pristine white suit and makes his way to a sports arena. There he finally sees Carmen, the woman he last saw 20 years ago before he was sent to prison. He wants her to go with him, but she has moved on with her life and married a police officer. Her husband sees them talking and tells Carlos that he will turn a blind eye if Carlos leaves.

Saddened that his dream reunion with Carmen has gone wrong, Carlos takes Lucky and Mac to the hidden gold, which happens to be stashed at the power station they had visited earlier. They unearth the bullion and head for their boat. El Gato Negro traps them as they try to head out to sea but Lucky lures him into a minefield and to his death. The threesome head off to sea, but are spotted by Cuban patrol boats. In the skirmish Carlos is shot dead and the boat badly damaged. Lucky and Mac abandon ship, but are eventually rescued by a floating whorehouse... and they have kept hold of some of the gold.

Background: "For me this film was another nightmare. My divorce had cost me dearly and I hadn't taken account of my tax position, so I had to earn some money. I was offered this not very good script called *Florida Straits*, but it had one redeeming feature. It was going to be shot in Mexico, a country which I loved.

"So I went to Mexico and found all of the locations. Everything seemed fine, then the producers rang to say they couldn't afford to shoot in Mexico. Couldn't afford to shoot in Mexico? Worse, they wanted to shoot in North Carolina and would I go and look at it.

"So, here we had a film where virtually the whole story is set in the jungles of Cuba. Not only that, there is a sea battle off the coast of Cuba and they wanted me to shoot in the Carolinas. It was incredible.

"I flew out there to take a look. It was pouring with rain the whole time and the place looked like Wiltshire. I couldn't believe it. But the producers were adamant and, to this day, I don't know the real reason behind this crazy decision. They had done a deal with a studio in Shelby, which is a replica of Peyton Place, and everything was in place. I was trapped - I had spent eight months of my life planning this film, and there was no way I would be able to get another one to resolve my financial situation.

"So I had to bite the bullet. I agreed to shoot in the Carolinas if I could bring in my own team. That's what saved me. I brought in my old designer friend Voytek, camera team, editor, art department, even my two sons. I also had good actors in Raul Julia and Fred Ward.

"The shooting, while it was hard, was fun. Voytek and I had to be really inventive in the way we used the locations to look like Cuba. We put up billboards of Castro to hide things. We used peach orchards, fog machines, and a big bonus was the abandoned nuclear power station near the studio. Somehow I think we managed to pull it off and it was great working with Raul Julia, who was a terrific actor.

"But when we returned to LA and finished the cut they pulled me off the film. HBO said they were delighted but one of the producers, Robert Cooper, decided he wanted me out of the cutting room while they recut the film. The DGA (Directors' Guild of America) defended me but HBO stood by and let it happen. When Cooper fired my editor there was nothing I could do but return home. They then shot some additional scenes with a double of Julia - ridiculously the double was half his size! These useless scenes, shot in a fake Mexican village that happened to be standing on a backlot somewhere, were comedic. They also put on this awful music! I had found in New York, Spanish Harlem, all of this amazing Cuban music. But all of that was ripped off and replaced with brainless synthesiser shit."

Themes/Subtext: Though brought on board as a director for hire, the politics behind *Florida Straits* were of most interest to Mike Hodges, rather than the more traditional tale of three men on the hunt for gold. The prospect of tackling a story even partially set in Cuba allowed him to draw on his days as a documentary filmmaker with *World In Action*, and the socialist in him enjoyed poking fun at abortive interventions by America in Cuba. The fact that much of the action takes place in an abandoned power station which in the story had been initially funded by the US allowed Hodges to stage a modest attack on US foreign policies.

The Verdict: The bold intention to stage an updated *To Have And Have Not* is patently clear, but sadly so are the limitations of the budget and some of the ham-fisted alterations made by the producers. Raul Julia and Fred Ward are just fine in the lead roles, and some of the locations work extremely well, but this remains an intriguing telemovie that doesn't really stand shoulder to shoulder with Hodges' other films.

10. Prayers And Memories

A Prayer For The Dying (1987)

Cast: Mickey Rourke (Martin Fallon), Bob Hoskins (Father Da Costa), Alan Bates (Jack Meehan), Sammi Davis (Anna), Christopher Fulford (Billy Meehan), Liam Neeson (Liam Docherty), Leonard Termo (Bonati), Camille Coduri (Jenny), Maurice O'Connell (Miller), Allson Doody (Siobhan Donovan), Anthony Head (Rupert).

Crew: Director Mike Hodges, Screenwriters Edmund Ward & Martin Lynch, Novel Jack Higgins, Producers Samuel Goldwyn Jr. & Peter Snell, Cinematographer Mike Garfath, Editor Peter Boyle, Production Designer Evan Hercules, Art Director Martyn Herbert, Costumes Evangeline Harrison. 103 minutes.

(Note: version viewed was Mike Hodges' original cut, hopefully to be reassembled for DVD release.)

Story: In the green fields of Northern Ireland, IRA man Martin Fallon is part of a team setting a pipe bomb to blow up a British Army Land Rover. Unfortunately, the Land Rover is overtaken by a school bus full of young children and, to Fallon's horror, he watches in the distance as the bus explodes. Fallon is mortified, leaves Northern Ireland and heads to Canning Town in London where he can get a new passport.

To achieve this, however, he has to kill one more time. He refuses. Meanwhile, Fallon's IRA friend Liam Docherty arrives in London to track him down, and is met by local IRA contact Siobhan Donovan. Finally realising that his only way out is to carry out the hit on gangster Cresco, rival of the undertaker-cum-crime boss Jack Meehan.

Fallon does the hit but is seen by the local priest, Father Da Costa. Before the priest can give evidence to the police, Fallon confesses his sins to Da Costa, who is then honour-bound not to tell anyone. Fallon is increasingly drawn to the priest and his blind niece, Anna, and when the police arrive at the church Fallon manages to keep his cover by pretending to tune the church's organ, which he plays beautifully.

To shut up the priest, Meehan sends his thugs to torch the church. However, Da Costa comes from a military background and he beats up Meehan's men. Docherty tracks down Fallon and asks him to return to Ireland, but Fallon refuses. Docherty draws a gun but can't bring himself to shoot his friend.

Fallon befriends Anna and takes her to a local funfair, watched by Meehan's thuggish brother Billy. After returning her home, Fallon leaves. Billy breaks into the house and torments Anna, spraying her face with red paint. When he tries to rape her she stabs him with a pair of scissors. Meanwhile, to punish Docherty's weakness, Siobhan Donovan assassinates him.

Jack Meehan plans to kill Da Costa and Anna by planting a bomb on the roof of the church. Fallon sneaks onto the roof and, in the ensuing fight, Meehan pushes Fallon through a hole in the roof. Fallon, dangling from a large cross, clings onto the figure of Christ, while Meehan struggles to defuse the bomb. It explodes, killing Meehan. Fallon eventually dies amidst the rubble of the church.

Background: Based on a novel by thriller writer Jack Higgins, who had prepared the first version of the script, this was originally to be directed by Franc Roddam. According to Mike Hodges, the script had been rewritten by Roddam, and Sam Goldwyn Jr. said it was an "extremely violent" version, and that's not what they wanted. "Quite rightly really," said Hodges, "the whole point of *A Prayer For The Dying* is that it is about a man turning his back on violence. I was told they had a million-dollar pay-or-play deal with Mickey Rourke, that he had another film coming up, so they had to get moving pretty rapidly.

"Even though I only had five weeks of preparation, I admired Mickey Rourke so much I decided to take the gamble. I managed to convince Bob Hoskins and Alan Bates - somewhat reluctantly because of the script - that it had potential, that we could make a good film."

The film was shot on location in Silvertown in East London, making use of a disused church as the key location spot, and allowing Mickey Rourke to dress as grungily as possible.

"What the producers didn't tell me were all the conditions of their contract with Mickey," added Hodges. "He had approval not only of director (luckily he had spoken to Nic Roeg who had put in a good word for me) but also cast approval of the priest, Da Costa, and the villain, Meehan, but, worst of all, approval of the actress to play Hoskins' blind niece.

"Mickey was seemingly attracted to leggy Californian models, which clearly wouldn't look right in a gloomy presbytery. Eventually we settled on Sammi Davis as someone who could be believable in the part. In the script there was a love scene between them, which I hated, and now he wanted it taken out. Fine by me. What we did instead was a touching scene where he cleans the red paint sprayed by Billy Meehan on her face. It was much better than any love scene but not for folks back in LA.

"I enjoyed shooting the film very much. Mickey had worked hard to master the Belfast accent, no easy job, and had managed it brilliantly. Sadly, as soon as we started filming Mickey took a dislike to Goldwyn's representative on the film. He wanted him banned from the set, he couldn't stand him watching, and I concurred. He was banned. Now we started getting feedback from LA. They couldn't understand Mickey's accent, and thought his performance was listless. They seemed incapable of understanding that Fallon was a man having a breakdown. They expected an IRA man to be like a Mafia hit man or something. Goldwyn was going demented. During all this, I was trying to get the film finished on time!" In the interests of seeking reality for his role, as well as perfecting his accent Rourke also wanted an IRA tattoo on his arm. Unfortunately he insisted on the real thing rather than a painless transfer. As Hodges pointed out: "Sadly, it went septic, presaging the film's fate."

Hodges added: "We were seeing really good rushes but Goldwyn just hated them. The best we could do was keep the Goldwyn people at bay until we finished the shoot. But I knew they would have their revenge eventually. I was right.

"Mickey was professional throughout and we finished the film on schedule and on budget. I edited, recorded the score and dubbed it. It was delivered to The Goldwyn Company on time. Back in California they drastically re-edited it, stripped the soundtrack off and saturated it with totally inappropriate music. It is not bad, I suppose, what they ended up with, but it is not the film I made, which I think is more interesting."

Hodges wouldn't let the situation rest and went public in his condemnation of the changes made to *A Prayer For The Dying*. He said: "It all got out of hand. My press release was meant for the trade press, *Variety* and *The Hollywood Reporter*. I wanted the industry to know that this wasn't the film I had handed over to Goldwyn. Unfortunately, the release went out to all the national papers, not just the trades. Somehow a rumour circulated that I wanted my name taken off because they had removed my pro-IRA ending - I have no idea where that came from!"

In an article he wrote for *Time Out* in November 1997 Hodges detailed further what happened after he submitted his print to Goldwyn. 'After numerous requests I was finally shown what Goldwyn Jr. has perpetrated in my name. The film had been completely re-edited, and a different music and soundtrack substituted. It was no longer the film I made. Worse, that trust between director and actor, in this case Hoskins and Bates, had been breached. Goldwyn later excused himself by saying the film was now "more acceptable to American audiences."'

More recently Hodges added: "Of course, by going public, no one in the industry wanted to know about me. Defend your films and you risk being branded as difficult. Be passionate about them and you're vulnerable. I learnt that throughout the 1980s. Three out of the last four had been taken away from me and recut.

"What angered me most about *A Prayer For The Dying* was that I had saved their bacon by taking the risk at that late stage. I had then managed, against the odds, to deliver it on schedule and on budget - and that's what they did to me. I had written to Sam Goldwyn twice suggesting we preview - and be guided by the audience reaction. He didn't even bother to reply. And it was a good film! The version they distributed in America died as surely as Fallon did in the film."

Hodges has recently been working with MGM, which controls the Goldwyn library, to restore *A Prayer For The Dying* to its original form for a DVD release. "The material they cut must be somewhere, we just have to find it. I would love to see it shown in its proper form. Looking at it again recently I was proud of what we managed to do. I think it's a really interesting film." The controversy surrounding the film reached its peak in November 1987. It had been chosen to open the London Film Festival, despite the fact that it was common knowledge Hodges wanted his name removed from the credits. Then, at short notice, the Festival director decided to pull it from its gala screening. Despite the fact that the film - even in the Goldwyn version - is clearly anti-terrorist, the LFF director Sheila Whitaker said that IRA killings in Northern Ireland a short time before had led to a situation where screening the film would be inappropriate.

Themes/Subtext: For Hodges - and despite what some critics said at the time - *A Prayer For The Dying* was never about celebrating violence. It was very much about examining how a man can turn his back on violence and try to redeem himself. The film also allowed him to dabble in two elements he had enjoyed working before: the gangland thriller, as seen in *Get Carter*; and the world of funeral directors, which had been the subject of one of his very first *World In Action* documentaries. As a lapsed Catholic, the film also allowed Hodges to delve into religion, and use Father Da Costa's concerns about his faith to reflect some of his own thoughts. The film, as with *Get Carter*, presents a violent loner (this time Mickey Rourke as the repentant IRA killer) adrift in an alien environment (East London as compared to the green hills of Northern Ireland). Unlike Carter, though, Rourke's Martin Fallon is no longer the cold-hearted killer. At the end Fallon has to die as atonement for his sins, though at least he has found some kind of peace, having saved lives rather than taken them.

The Verdict: *A Prayer For The Dying* offers a good deal to enjoy, especially in the form of Mickey Rourke's well-intentioned performance, which features an impressive Irish accent. Bob Hoskins looks a tad uncomfortable as a military man turned priest, but the seedy East London locations work extremely well and the murder sequences in the middle of the graveyard are very well staged. Released at a time when the IRA was still extremely active, it is easy to see why the film got a hard time from critics. There remain many interesting elements, and while the story betrays its literary origins, Hodges works hard to given the film greater depth than a simplistic action thriller. Worth another look.

Midnight Shakes The Memory (1988)

After the bad experience of *A Prayer For The Dying*, Hodges went on to write a script titled *Midnight Shakes The Memory*. "Some friends suggested we made a film about Orson Welles' stage production of *The Cradle Will Rock*. Welles was then 21, the toast of Broadway. But with this production things came unstuck. Government funding was suddenly withdrawn, and they were banned from using the theatre. This was just after the Great Depression. Instead of buckling under political pressure, they found another theatre and had the audience walk twenty blocks to the new venue. Meanwhile the producer, John Houseman, told the cast that, although they could not legally appear on stage, no law could stop them joining in the musical from among audience. This they did, and it was a triumph. It was a great story, and I agreed to do it with the proviso all the characters were clearly actors pretending to be Welles, Houseman and the others. I set all the action in a theatre and, as in *Squaring The Circle,* had characters talking to camera.

"I finished the script and it was good enough to attract Tim Robbins as Orson Welles, Alan Rickman as John Houseman and Jeff Goldblum as Marc Blitztein, the composer. Sadly the script frightened or puzzled the money people and the producers couldn't get it off the ground. Remember, at that time, the cast was pretty much unknown.

"A few years later I was in Los Angeles and visited Robert Altman on the set of *The Player*. I finally got to meet Tim Robbins - all of the negotiations had been done via agents - and asked him if he remembered my script. He told me how much he liked it, and still had his copy at home.

"When *The Player* became a box-office hit, I went back to the producers, pointing out that Robbins was now a star, so was Alan Rickman after *Truly, Madly, Deeply,* and suggested we go back to them and try again to get the film financed.

"Understandably, Alan said the role of Houseman was now too small for him, and Robbins said 'yes' but he wanted to write and direct it himself. When the producers asked if I would step aside, I agreed immediately. We had tried for like six years and, whilst I loved the script, I was sure Robbins would get it made. I had written the script for a token fee, $10,000, and assumed that I would now be paid a proper fee for my work. Oh yeah?

"I had used part of Houseman's autobiography in the script and had to get his permission to use it. Not long before he died he had read the script and gave it his blessing, which I found surprising because it was not flattering about him. For the rights we had to pay $10,000. The producers could only raise $5,000, and I ended up giving back half of my script fee to make up the shortfall. Now, years later, they wanted me to sign over my rights so that Robbins could make it - and they offered to repay me that $5,000! Again I was repaid with an attempt to screw me! I had them deal with my agent and, after a lot of haggling, I received a proper fee."

Hodges received no final credit on the completed film, *The Cradle Will Rock* (1999), and stresses he wouldn't want one. "I thought it was an awful mess. A great shame because the story has such simplicity. This was lost when Robbins stuffed it with superfluous characters like Rockefeller, Diego Rivera, Frida Kahlo - presumably to cast it up with famous friends. In the confusion I'm afraid the true story got lost."

11. Black Rainbow (1989)

Cast: Rosanna Arquette (Martha Travis), Jason Robards (Walter Travis), Tom Hulce (Gary Wallace), Mark Joy (Lloyd Harley), Ron Rosenthal (Irving Weinberg), John Bennes (Ted Silas), Linda Pierce (Mary Kuron).

Crew: Director Mike Hodges, Screenwriter Mike Hodges, Producers John Quested & Geoffrey Helman, Cinematographer Gerry Fisher, Editor Malcolm Cooke, Production Designer Voytek, Music John Scott, Art Director Patty Kawonn, Costumes Clifford Capone. 95 minutes.

Story: Reporter Gary Wallace tracks down Martha Travis, a reclusive medium now living in a small rural shack, who vanished 10 years earlier. He takes photos of her from a distance and then knocks on her door. He tells her he knows her from years earlier and wants to know what has happened since her father's murder. The story then goes back 10 years.

Martha and her father Walter Travis (who drinks heavily in secret) travel around the country by train, stopping at small towns to stage spiritualist events. These are all staged in crumbling American towns and attended by ordinary folk who have a deep-rooted faith in God. During one performance she apparently receives a message from Tom Kuron, a murdered man, to pass on to his wife Mary who is in the audience. But Kuron is not dead. In fact his wife left him watching the televisions just a short while earlier.

Later that evening, Mary tells her husband about the medium's prophecy about his murder and her vision of the blood spattered around their sitting room. Mary goes into the kitchen to make a drink and, while Tom sits on the sofa, a man appears at the windows and sprays bullets into the room, killing Tom.

Young reporter Gary Wallace arrives at the crime scene, and hears about Martha's prediction from a neighbour. The neighbour also tells Wallace that he suspects the killing was linked to Kuron's plans to blow the whistle on health and safety violations at the local Silas chemical plant, which employs many of the townspeople.

Wallace tracks Martha and her father to the next town and proceeds to ply Walter with alcohol. He then beds Martha to get more information on the story. At the same time, in a scene shot with delicious irony, the hit man gets a call saying that he has another job: the medium. The hit man is shown living a stable family life, having breakfast with his wife and three children with a small Christmas tree visible in the background

At the next session Martha proceeds to frighten the audience by reciting a long list of names of people claiming they are speaking to her from the afterlife. Again they are all still alive. The next morning an explosion wrecks a chemical works. Again Martha's prophecy has been fulfilled. Wallace goes to the factory to interview the people waiting for news of their loved ones.

As Martha prepares for the evening session, the hit man arrives in town and, after checking out the theatre she is using, heads to the hotel where Martha and her father are staying. On stage that night, Martha starts to 'perform' and asks if anyone in the audience knows a Walt or a Walter. With a scream she realises it is her own father talking to her from 'over there.'

Back at the hotel, the drunken Walter sees a vision of Martha and is terrified. He sneaks into the corridor to escape but the hit man hears him. Now the hit man sees the same vision of Martha, but when he shoots the bullets pass through her and hit Walter. The police kill the murderer as he tries to make a getaway.

Back to the present day, and Gary Wallace confronts his editor with the photographs of the now reclusive Martha and insists that he has a story. When the pictures are developed they show nothing but a ramshackle house, covered with foliage. It is clear that it is not lived in. There is no sign of Martha at all.

Background: Following his disappointments of the late 1980s, Hodges decided to write another script rather than rely on being offered projects, so he wrote *Black Rainbow* on spec. He went to his agent Terence Baker (actor George Baker's brother, now deceased) with the script, and Baker in turn took it to John

Quested, then head of Goldcrest Films. At that time in the late 1980s, Goldcrest was a rather different company that the production outfit that had made (famously) *Chariots Of Fire* and (notoriously) *Revolution*, and was looking to slowly relaunch itself.

"Terence was having lunch with John Quested, and asked John what sort of projects Goldcrest was looking for," said Hodges. "He said he was for a story like *Elmer Gantry*, the old Jean Simmons/Burt Lancaster film about an evangelist preacher. Terence told him he happened to have just the script.

"The whole experience, thank goodness, of working with Goldcrest and making *Black Rainbow* was quite wonderful. Very interesting that the film had a big, big role for a woman. One is always hearing that there are no good roles for women, and yet I had a terrible time getting anyone to play it. Eventually Rosanna Arquette read it - thanks to Martin Scorsese who had worked with her - and she took it on straight away.

"The one good thing to come from *Florida Straits* was memories of the extraordinary locations in the Carolinas. They brought me back to Edward Hopper - the towns and countryside there is perfect Hopper territory. When I wrote the script I was very much influenced by what I had taken in while making *Florida Straits*. However, when I went back, particularly to Charlotte, much of it had been demolished. I eventually had to build hotel rooms because all the old hotels had gone. Like in *Get Carter*, I had caught a town losing its identity. This time I was nearly too late.

"All my scripts are grounded in research. This time I had noticed in the local newspapers reports on workers and foremen being beaten up and sometimes killed - and that there was often a link to factory safety. Not just in the Carolinas - I had collected similar news cuttings on my travels all over the US. Basically the employees were being done over by the bosses when they threatened to spill the beans.

"That was the starting point. And it tied into my concerns about the cavalier way we are eating up our natural resources and despoiling the amazing planet we inhabit. It genuinely puzzles me why we are so dumb. I also needed a character who was a seer, someone to warn us of the consequences of what we're doing. Then I came up with the idea of a stage medium - someone who could be a fraud or could have a genuine power of prophecy. Let the audiences decide. That appealed to me. So all of the elements came together and I wrote about someone who supposedly communicates with the dead. In a sense we all do that."

Black Rainbow was shot on location in North Carolina in just six weeks with a budget of $7 million. Hodges brought the film in on schedule and had the happy - and this was unusual for him in the 1980s - experience of being able to complete, edit and score the film exactly as he intended. But naturally there had to be problems. "It was never distributed in the US. It went straight to cable television. Miramax promised a theatrical release, but didn't keep their promise. It's not uncommon in the film industry.

"Back in the UK there were also distribution problems in the UK. Despite great reviews it was dumped in the toilet. Palace Pictures, the distributors, were going broke, only we didn't know it. They needed quick money and had sold it to a video company. So, whilst the film was the way I had wanted it, the distribution was disastrous." The film, though, did screen at the 22nd Sitges Fantasy Film Festival in October 1989, where it won the Best Screenplay award for Hodges and the Best Actress award for Rosanna Arquette. Speaking in *Cinefantastique* Hodges said of Arquette: "Rosanna was brave to do it. Many actresses would, did, turn the role down. I had a lot of problems getting a star name but Rosanna took it on - and at very short notice. Initially she had great difficulty with the act. She emoted too much - but that's exactly how I'd written it. When performed I knew my script was wrong. I had shot the scene in front of a real audience and they were deeply moved, some were crying. Next morning we had a horrible row and she was going to quit. She kept saying 'but they were crying.' Somehow I talked her into starting again. From then it was just fine. Rosanna gave the role the toughness every entertainer on the road has. To her, it's a job. Being a seer was her curse. Rosanna was extra wonderful because the little-girl-lost character that emerged was beyond and above my original intentions."

Themes/Subtext: It was Hodges' obsession with the exploitation of people by spiritualism and new-age religions that prompted him to develop *Black Rainbow*. The story also enabled him to link in his socialist politics yet again - the film shows how some big industrial companies treat their workforce. Much of this came from his experiences while making a *World In Action* documentary on American unions many years before. The film, therefore, is a blend of the supernatural, religion and politics, with a dose of crime thriller thrown in for good measure (Arquette 'sees' the killer and, in turn, has to be murdered).

Hodges' metaphor for the creeping power of both corrupt corporations and a life-force that exists above all human endeavours comes in the form of the weed 'kudzu'. The very first scene in the film concerns kudzu. "Kudzu. Goddamned kudzu. You know we can't kill that stuff. Nothing known to man can stop it. Poisons. Pesticides. They even tried flame throwers." The Japanese weed was introduced into America at the turn of the century, apparently to bind the raised railway lines. Known as 'foot-a-day' the weed got out of control and started to cover the land, and climb every building in its path. "It's moving north, you know. Inch by inch. One day it'll reach New York." Hodges had noticed this weed in his travels on America's east coast. It is also worth noting that, finally, he had written a strong female role and, despite the crime elements, at the core *Black Rainbow* is a supernatural thriller glued together by brilliant performances.

The Verdict: Dominic Wells in *Time Out* wrote that *Black Rainbow* contained: 'Superbly understated performances – Hodges' best film since *Get Carter*, a psychological thriller with a brain and a heart.' It is disgraceful that this intriguing and fascinating film has never received the exposure it deserved. Rosanna Arquette gives a quite wonderful performance as the medium (at times sad, then sexy and then troubled) who talks with 'spirit' voices before they have actually died, and Jason Robards is perfect as her alcoholic father. The story is terrific and the locations evocative. *Black Rainbow* is an supernatural thriller well worth tracking down.

12. Interlude III: Back Into Television

Dandelion Dead (1994)

Cast: Michael Kitchen (Major Herbert Armstrong), Sarah Miles (Katherine Armstrong), David Thewlis (Oswald Martin), Lesley Sharp (Connie Davies), Peter Vaughan (Tom Hinicks), Diana Quick (Marion Glassford-Gale), Bernard Hepton (Davies), Robert Stephens (Vaughan), Chloe Tucker (Eleanor), Roger Lloyd Pack (Phillips), Alexandra Milma (Margaret), Joseph Steel (Pearson).

Crew: Director Mike Hodges, Screenwriter Michael Chaplin, Producer Patrick Harbinson, Executive Producer Sarah Wilson, Cinematographer Gerry Fisher, Production Designer Voytek, Music Barrington Pheloung, Editor Malcolm Cooke. LWT (London Weekend Television). Transmitted: February 6 & 13, 1994. Running times: Part I - 111 minutes, Part II - 103 minutes.

Story: *Dandelion Dead* is based on a true-life murder story that was the sensation of 1921, set against the backdrop of small-town rural life. Major Herbert Armstrong is a stiff upper lip English gentleman who also happens to be a lawyer, but whose good humour is much strained by the constant nagging of his wife Katherine. By the end of Part One she is no longer around, having been killed with the arsenic Armstrong uses to deal with the dandelions ruining his lawn. Part Two deals more with the investigation, court case, eventual guilty verdict and execution of Major Armstrong.

Background: *Dandelion Dead* is a four-hour television film, made for LWT and shown in two parts. "I was thinking what I wanted to do next, and decided I really wanted to do a rural thriller, like *Suspect*, which had been my first film. I had even started reading the crime books of Simenon again - I had always loved them - and along came *Dandelion Dead*. The script was just wonderful and I agreed to do it immediately. There were no horror stories with *Dandelion Dead* whatsoever. It was a thoroughly enjoyable experience with an excellent cast. I hadn't done any television since *Squaring The Circle*, so it was interesting to go back and see how the process had changed.

"Back when I made *Suspect* and *Rumour*, once the script was approved, that was it. They let me get on with it. No one even asked me who I had cast in it. Nowadays television producers are obsessed with having every role, however small, filled with a 'name' actor. Every show is like Madame Tussaud's. One thing, however, hasn't changed - television directors still get no residuals. For them, television has become a sweatshop.

"And some of the producers are very inexperienced. Here I was making a story set in 1919, in Hay-on-Wye, a small country town, with two solicitors' offices facing each other across the street, an element vital to the story. I asked how much time they'd allocated to shooting in Hay. One week, was the reply, seven in London. London?

"I was rather surprised and suggested they switch the balance of the shooting schedule to Hay but with the same budget constraints. They came back with five weeks in Hay and two in London - reducing the total shoot by one week. That made them very nervous. But it was obvious that just getting around in London with a crew could eat up a week, as well as the time we'd lose from aircraft noise and cars. No one had really thought it through.

"So we had a good shoot in Hay-on-Wye and made this cracking film. It was a lovely film to work on. I enjoyed it very much."

The Lifeforce Experiment (1994)

Cast: Donald Sutherland (Dr James Maclean), Mimi Kuzyk (Jessica Saunders), Corin Nemec (Ken), Hayley Reynolds (Nikki), Vlasta Vrana, Miguel Fernandes, Michael Rudder, Michael Reynolds, Bronwen Mantel.

Crew: Director Piers Haggard, Screenwriter Mike Hodges, Short Story *The Breakthrough* Daphne du Maurier, Producer Nicolas Clermont, Cinematographer Peter Benison, Production Designer John Meighen, Editor Yves Langlois, Music Osvaldo Montes. Sci-Fi Channel, First aired April 16, 1994.

Story: Dr James Maclean is a rumpled genius of a scientist engaging in dubious experiments in his laboratory in outer Newfoundland. Jessica Saunders is the CIA agent who is sent to find out exactly what Mac is up to with the agency's research money, and finds that he has developed a device for capturing and storing the energy of people's life-force on the point of death.

Background: *The Lifeforce Experiment* screened in the US as the Sci-Fi Channel's Planetary Premiere Movie. Mike Hodges was originally going to direct but didn't like the script changes being suggested. They were moving further and further from du Maurier's original story (one of the stories in the *Don't Look Now* edition) and he finally declined to direct.

The Healer (1994)

Cast: Paul Rhys (Dr John Lassiter), Geraldine James (Dr Mercedes Honeysett), Julie Covington (Madeleine Harland), Michael Britton (Simon Major), Richard Lynch (Save Major), Melanie Waters (Gill Major), Nicky Henson (Dr Ralph Raebryte), Fraser James (Jack Dark), Hilary Mason (Mary Simpson).

Crew: Director Mike Hodges, Screenwriter GF Newman, Producers GF Newman & Clive Brill, Editor John Richards, Executive Producers Ruth Caleb & Michael Wearing. A BBC Production. Transmitted in two parts on September 19 & 20, 1994. 110 minutes.

Story: Dr John Lassiter, a newly-employed house officer at Sparrow Hill Teaching Hospital, gradually comes to realise he possesses the gift of healing people simply through touch. Soon, though, he becomes trapped in a dual role as a medical man and a miracle worker. When the news gets out, it all turns into something of a circus: his colleagues see him as a threat to medicine; the media want to expose him as a fraud; and the public wants miracles on demand. Such is the ensuing confusion that the one miracle he actually pulls off goes unnoticed by everybody.

Background: "This was my one and only experience of working with the BBC. It was scripted by GF Newman, who had written *Law And Order* in the late 1970s, which I really admired. I liked the idea of *The Healer* very much, and accepted the offer with alacrity. We shot it on location in Merthyr Tydfil. Sadly GF Newman and I fell out on the first day of shooting. He interfered at one point with my direction, in front of the crew, which is unpardonable. I immediately rang my agent and said I wouldn't continue unless he was banned from the set.

"When I took on the project they neglected to tell me that Newman was one of the producers. If I had known this I probably wouldn't have become involved because it can only lead to creative problems. And it did when it came to editing the film.

"The climax of the piece is the 'miracle' the doctor actually performs but which goes unnoticed. I shot it all terribly simply because I knew that if I elaborated it simply wouldn't be believable. Just read the miracles in the *New Testament*. All the descriptions are plain and simple. 'He picked up his bed and walked.' And that was my inspiration. The doctor picks this young man up, he has fallen from his wheelchair, and puts him back in the chair. He walks off and never even sees the paraplegic's twisted limbs just unravel, like a flower opening up in the morning. It was raining when I shot this scene. I had the camera pan off the young man to a tree. It so happened that as it reached the tree the sun came out and a light wind made the leaves shimmer. It was quite magical.

"But Newman wasn't satisfied. He wanted to sentimentalise the miracle, he wanted Puccini playing all over it, he wanted the paraplegic, now with perfect shining teeth, to get up and perform a jeté in slow motion. It was completely wrong, mad, laughable.

"I had made the film on a very small budget. It seems the BBC had subsequently got an overseas sale and, to my astonishment, allowed this money to be spent so that Newman could go out and reshoot. Needless to say it was a complete waste of money, public money to boot. The version eventually transmitted was mine - so it worked out in the end! Another storm in a teacup."

In 1991 Hodges wrote two unproduced scripts (*Tiger Rag* and *Maiden*) and later, he also wrote *Warriors In Eden* (1992) for Goldcrest Films and *Acid Casuals* (1996), based on the novel by Nicholas Blincoe. Neither of the projects ever made it to production. Hodges directed Henry Purcell's opera *Dido And Aeneas* for the Abbotsbury Music Festival in 1997. In the same year he wrote his second stage play, *Shooting Stars & Other Heavenly Pursuits*.

13. Endgame - And New Beginnings

Croupier (1998)

Cast: Clive Owen (Jack Manfred), Gina McKee (Marion Neil), Alex Kingston (Jani de Villiers), Alexander Morton (David Reynolds), Kate Hardie (Bella), Paul Reynolds (Matt), Nick Reding (Giles Cremorne), Nicholas Ball (Jack Sr.), Ozzi Yue (Mr Tchai).

Crew: Director Mike Hodges, Writer Paul Mayersberg, Producer Jonathan Cavendish, Executive Producer James Mitchell, Cinematographer Mike Garfath, Editor Les Healey, Composer Simon Fisher Turner, Production Designer Jon Bunker, Costume Designer Caroline Harris. 89 minutes.

Story: Jack Manfred is a would-be writer whose first novel has been rejected. He gets a phone call from his father, a lifelong gambler now working in South Africa, who has set up an interview for Jack at a London casino. Jack had been brought up on the circuit in South Africa, is trained as a croupier by his father, but is reluctant to get back into the casino world. However, he needs a job and the money that goes with it. Jack impresses the casino manager David Reynolds and, after offering Jack a job, he explains the ground rules - friendships between croupiers are discouraged and it is forbidden to talk to a punter outside the casino.

Jack lives with Marion, his girlfriend, an ex-policewoman now a store detective, and she is surprised and a little concerned that he will now be working nights at the casino. She wants him to concentrate on his writing. One night at the Casino Jani de Villiers gambles at Jack's table. She is a shrewd South African gambler and impresses Jack in the way she quits the game while ahead. That same night, Jack spots a fellow croupier Matt cheating, and tells him if he sees him doing it again he'll report him.

Jack later bumps into Jani de Villiers at a London hotel and, against the rules, has a drink with her. He finds they have a lot in common: a background in South Africa and an understanding of the casino world. On another evening he is attacked in the street by a man he had caught cheating. He is pulled away from the fight by fellow croupier Bella, and they end up spending the night together. All these experiences prompt Jack to start writing again, this time telling the story of a croupier - himself. Marion reads it and finds the story too dark, without hope. Bella turns up at his flat and accuses him of getting her fired.

Later Jack bumps into an old publisher friend Giles, who invites him to a house party over the weekend. Jack asks Jani to go with him, but during a platonic night in their room he finds out she is not all she appears to be. She owes a lot of money and begs Jack to help her. She is involved with a gang of criminals who plan to rob the casino, but they need an inside man. Jack refuses to help. Jani offers him £10,000, with more to come when the job is over. Despite his refusal, Jack mulls over what he could do with the money and changes his mind. Marion, though, accidentally finds the money and, after overhearing a phone message from Jani, gets suspicious.

On the night of the robbery the attempt is foiled when the police arrive. Someone had tipped them and the casino off. Jack is in the clear but Marion still suspects his involvement. She confronts him and gives him an ultimatum: quit the casino job or she will tell the police about his part in the heist. Jack goes back to his book. One night the police arrive at the flat. Marion has been killed - accidentally knocked down by a passing car. Full of guilt, Jack finishes his novel.

His book, shrewdly titled *I, Croupier*, is published anonymously and is a best-seller with Jack now earning loads of money. But there remains one final twist, one more clever throw of the dice. Jack receives a phone call from Jani in South Africa. She and his father Jack Sr. are to be married. In the end, it turns out that Jack's father had been dealing the cards all of the time - and from the bottom of the pack.

Background: "David Aukin was running FilmFour at the time I was offered *Croupier*. Strangely enough, he had put on my first stage play *Soft Shoe Shuffle* at the Leicester Haymarket and the

Lyric Hammersmith in 1985, before he went to the National Theatre.

"Aukin knew the writer Paul Mayersberg, who had gone to him with the script idea that would turn out to be *Croupier*. I think that Paul had done about six drafts by then and, though it still wasn't right, it was ready enough to think about a director.

"And thank goodness they came up with my name. As soon as I read it, I couldn't believe my luck. An adult, intelligent script at last! I liked the whole premise of it. It wasn't really about gambling at all! It was about everything! The existentialists often used gambling as a metaphor but Paul had given it a new twist. It reflected life as most of us live it now, stripped of ideology and beliefs. And we think we have everything under control, with our computers, our electronic diaries, mobile phones, fast cars, life insurance, house and accident and medical cover. Even our pets are insured. Every second of our lives is accounted for - then something happens, like being hit by car or cancer - and the whole thing disintegrates. We forget how vulnerable we really are.

"So I leapt at it! FilmFour had gone to a production house (because they don't make films in-house themselves) called Little Bird, and I met with the producer Jonathan Cavendish. Paul and I then worked for about six months on the script and all sorts of changes worked their way into the storyline.

"The voice-over was always there, but its schizophrenic quality was added in later. I kept saying that I didn't believe the lead character was a writer, so we had to work on making the story as much about being a writer as being a croupier. Also, Paul had done certain things that I felt were wrong. For example, Jack's flat was on the first floor, while I felt he should be in the basement where there's no natural light, like in the casino which is also below street level.

"In fact, no natural light falls on the croupier during the entire film. Even the tennis game, which in the script was a day scene, I set at night under floodlights. You only see the sky very briefly at the end of the film when there are scenes set in South Africa. It is literally an 'underground' film.

"While Paul and I were working together he came up with the idea of switching the voice-over to the third person - a major change that. He also thought of using the Jack's experiences in the casino as the motivation to return to his novel. So all of those elements started to fit together with both of us working on the script. Paul did all the writing, with me providing much of the visual interpretation. I loved the whole process."

Paul Mayersberg added: "The origin of the film is a curious one. I had for many years tried to write a film about a gambler who plans a raid on a casino, but on the night of the robbery he breaks the bank himself and so there is no money to steal. I could never quite make it work as the story was an anticlimax. I decided to look at it from another angle - to tell a story where fate intervenes to ruin the plans but good comes of it. If you gamble you are aware of winning and losing streaks. In the original there was a character who never spoke, he was just an observer - the croupier. I decided to tell his story. I switched everything around and the croupier became the hero. The minor character became central and the gambler disappeared.

"I was inspired by Kurosawa's samurai story *The Hidden Fortress*, in which the lead characters are hangers-on. In Japan, many attitudes are the complete reversal of European attitudes. I took what I thought was a Japanese view of the story. I just kept the essence of the original ironic tale."

Though FilmFour was the lead company in the project, the financing structure (the film was budgeted at £3 million) meant that a good deal of the budget actually came from Germany. Production company Little Bird structured the funding between FilmFour and WDW/WDR in Germany with German production company Tatfilm, which had previously co-produced the BBC drama *The Writing On The Wall*. "That German money had to be spent in Germany," said Hodges, "Which I thought was great - I figured we could go to Berlin and use studios there. I then found out that as part of the deal we had to shoot in Düsseldorf. Luckily, we found a studio that was just the right size to build the casino and Jack's flat." Shooting took place at Mannheim studio, with the casino built over three weeks by production designer Jon Bunker.

"I had been concerned about the look of the casino," said Hodges. "The ones I looked at in London were visually pretty boring. Then one day I was on a 23 bus going down Oxford Street in London and the vast HMV store loomed into sight. It had a wonderful staircase lined with mirrors. That was it. Mirrors I thought to myself. They would give it lots of atmosphere - and enhance the sense of illusion, of things not being what they seem. Of course, they drove the camera crew crazy, keeping themselves and the lights out of every shot was not easy. We shot the whole film in 32 days. I managed to find a flow of simplicity in the way I shot it which was very pleasing for me. My main preoccupation as I get older is finding simplicity in my direction."

Production designer Jon Bunker added: "Mike wanted to convey that sense of purgatory so making the walls out of mirrors gives a sense of the casino extending forever. It also has the effect that when Jack enters the casino, the reflection in the mirror conveys the idea of him walking away from himself."

"Clive Owen as the croupier was brilliant to work with," added Mike Hodges. "I asked him to learn the voice-over in advance so that when he played each scene he would be responding to his own thoughts. And this meant I could keep the flow I'm talking about, knowing the voice-over would fit exactly. Clive never let me down. His precision was daunting."

"I liked the emotional world underneath the surface of the script," Clive Owen commented, "Which is not immediately apparent. It's very economically written with quite a simple storyline. The casino is an analogy for something bigger. The voice-over is the film for me. Without that, it would be too elusive. Jack has a conversation with the audience throughout. Part of my decision was also Mike's involvement. He's a joy to work with. He's very experienced which is very important when you're making such a complex film."

Themes/Subtext: As with previous films, *Croupier* is essentially about a loner thrust into a strange environment. Though Clive

Owen's dealer Jack Manfred has been a croupier before, he has never experienced the underground world of the London casinos, and while he doesn't really resort to violence, like Jack Carter he quietly observes what is going on around him. The design of the casino exploits the use of mirrors, which in turn distort both Jack's and the audience's view of events, further enhancing the dispassionate nature of the croupier. As Manfred comments at the close of proceedings when the film returns to the opening scene: "Now he had become the still centre of that spinning wheel of misfortune. The world turned around him, leaving him mysteriously untouched. The croupier had reached his goal: He no longer heard the sound of the ball." Paul Mayersberg's script makes extensive use of voice-over narration and this device suits the emotionally reticent lead character, offering important insight into Manfred's psyche.

The Verdict: Andrew Sarris in *The New York Observer* wrote of *Croupier*: 'One of the niftiest noir character studies to come along in a long time. Mike Hodges is one of the most underappreciated masters of the medium.' Kevin Thomas in *The Los Angeles Times* wrote: 'A work of compelling aplomb. *Croupier* is arguably Mike Hodges' finest film.' The film remains something of an oddity in terms of contemporary film-making. It is a thoughtful and intelligent movie that is part drama and part thriller, and cannot be easily bracketed. It doesn't rely on snappy pace or sharp editing, but rather moves languidly as it attempts to draw in the viewer rather than overwhelm one with effects. The fact that it has been such a critical and commercial success speaks volumes about what audiences really want compared to what film distributors sometimes think they want. It should also be said that critics love the chance to try and 'rescue' a film from what they perceive as abandonment by distributors - it would have been interesting to have seen how the film would have been received if given a full release right at the start. All power to FilmFour for giving the film a second chance - something that happens all too rarely these days.

14. Afterword

The critical impact of *Croupier*, as well as its slow financial success, has led to Mike Hodges being somewhat busier at the start of the new century than at many other times in his career.

His play *Shooting Stars & Other Heavenly Pursuits* (which he wrote in 1997) was staged in at the Old Red Lion, a 60-seat pub theatre in Islington, north London, in mid-2001, with Hodges also handling the directing chores. It was his first time as a theatre director. Appropriately enough, it is a play about the humour and madness of the movie business, with the action all taking place outside the suite of a superstar actor in a luxury hotel. Hodges wrote in *The Guardian* newspaper: 'It's based on my experiences in the film industry during the late 1970s and 1980s. Painful at the time, they are funny in retrospect. As Hitchcock once said to an over-exercised actor: "It is only a film." That said, my litany of failure, mostly at the hands of North Americans, is long.'

The success of *Croupier*, as Hodges happily admits, has made him hot again. Retrospectives of his work have been staged at the American Cinematheque in Los Angeles and at the Museum of Modern Art in New York. As Hodges wryly noted, the reviews have "promoted" him from "cult to veteran director."

He is working with actor Clive Owen again on a new feature, *I'll Sleep When I'm Dead*, scripted by Trevor Preston, which is to shoot in London and South Wales over 36 days on a $6 million budget. He is hoping to shoot early 2002. Hodges hopes to make the Thomas Mann story 'Mario And The Magician' from a script by the late Abraham Polonsky (*Force Of Evil*). FilmFour has commissioned Paul Mayersberg to write a script from a Hodges treatment titled *Hatchet Man*. He is also working on his own script *Grist*, and has completed a documentary on serial killer films *Murder By Numbers*. He has also been approached by MGM to restore *A Prayer For The Dying* to its original form for a possible DVD release. Not only are things looking good for the future, but he is also being given the rare chance to sort out problems from the past.

15. Reference Materials

Books

There are no other books about Mike Hodges. This is the first!

Magazines And Newspapers Consulted

Variety, The Hollywood Reporter, Screen International, The Guardian, The Daily Telegraph, The Los Angeles Times, USA Today, The New York Times, Village Voice, Chicago Sun-Times, Film Review, Time Out, Cinema Rising, Empire, Crime Time, American Cinematographer, Cinefantastique, Starburst

Videos

PAL
And The Ship Sails On (*E La Nave Va*) FC002
Black Rainbow TVT1147 (widescreen)
Damien: Omen II (as part Omen Trilogy box set) 8976C
Flash Gordon 783523
Flash Gordon 74321445723 (widescreen)
Florida Straits - deleted
Get Carter S050289
Get Carter S065482 (widescreen)
Morons From Outer Space - deleted
A Prayer For The Dying - deleted
The Terminal Man - deleted

NTSC
The Hitchhiker. Vol 1. (Containing W.G.O.D)
Black Rainbow
Damien: Omen II
Flash Gordon
Get Carter

Morons From Outer Space
A Prayer For The Dying
The Terminal Man

DVDs

And The Ship Sails On (region 1)
Damien: Omen II (region 1)
Flash Gordon (region 1)
Get Carter (region 2)

Websites

The Get Carter Site - www.btinternet.com/~ms.dear/carterindex.htm - Quite interesting fan site that clearly has lots of love for the film and a good deal of ambition, which is yet to be totally fulfilled. It offers a tempting taster to the film, and allows fans to indulge in some of those more famous *Get Carter* quotes.

The Flash Gordon Site - www.geocities.com/hollywood/4262 - Another enthusiastic fan site, which is mainly an assembly of images from the film and a list of favourite quotes.

The Omen Site - www.geocities.com/omenchronicles - An impressive site dealing with all of the *Omen* movies. It has a nice look at *Damien: Omen II*, though the film does not garner as much attention as the other *Omen* efforts.

The Croupier Site - www.filmfour.com/croupier - Has credits, background information and various other interesting bits and pieces. Usual film promotional site - how long it will be there is not clear.

The Essential Library

Build up your library with new titles every month

Alfred Hitchcock by Paul Duncan

More than 20 years after his death, Alfred Hitchcock is still a household name, most people in the Western world have seen at least one of his films, and he popularised the action movie format we see every week on the cinema screen. He was both a great artist and dynamite at the box office. This book examines the genius and enduring popularity of one of the most influential figures in the history of the cinema!

Stanley Kubrick by Paul Duncan

Kubrick's work, like all masterpieces, has a timeless quality. His vision is so complete, the detail so meticulous, that you believe you are in a three-dimensional space displayed on a two-dimensional screen. He was commercially successful because he embraced traditional genres like War (*Paths Of Glory*, *Full Metal Jacket*), Crime (*The Killing*), Science Fiction (*2001*), Horror (*The Shining*) and Love (*Barry Lyndon*). At the same time, he stretched the boundaries of film with controversial themes: underage sex (*Lolita*); ultra violence (*A Clockwork Orange*); and erotica (*Eyes Wide Shut*).

Orson Welles by Martin Fitzgerald

The popular myth is that after the artistic success of *Citizen Kane* it all went downhill from there for Orson Welles, that he was some kind of fallen genius. Yet, despite overwhelming odds, he went on to make great Films Noirs like *The Lady From Shanghai* and *Touch Of Evil*. He translated Shakespeare's work into films with heart and soul (*Othello*, *Chimes At Midnight*, *Macbeth*), and he refused to take the bite out of modern literature, giving voice to bitterness, regret and desperation in *The Magnificent Ambersons* and *The Trial*. Far from being down and out, Welles became one of the first cutting-edge independent filmmakers.

Film Noir by Paul Duncan

The laconic private eye, the corrupt cop, the heist that goes wrong, the femme fatale with the rich husband and the dim lover - these are the trademark characters of Film Noir. This book charts the progression of the Noir style as a vehicle for film-makers who wanted to record the darkness at the heart of American society as it emerged from World War to the Cold War. As well as an introduction explaining the origins of Film Noir, seven films are examined in detail and an exhaustive list of over 500 Films Noirs are listed.

The Essential Library

Currently Available

Film Directors:

Woody Allen (£3.99)

Jane Campion (£2.99)

Jackie Chan (£2.99)

David Cronenberg (£3.99)

Alfred Hitchcock (£3.99)

Stanley Kubrick (£2.99)

David Lynch (£3.99)

Sam Peckinpah (£2.99)

Orson Welles (£2.99)

Steven Spielberg (£3.99)

Tim Burton (£3.99)

John Carpenter (£3.99)

Joel & Ethan Coen (£3.99)

Terry Gilliam (£2.99)

Krzysztof Kieslowski (£2.99)

Sergio Leone (£3.99)

Brian De Palma (£2.99)

Ridley Scott (£3.99)

Billy Wilder (£3.99)

Film Genres:

Film Noir (£3.99)

Horror Films (£3.99)

Spaghetti Westerns (£3.99)

Blaxploitation Films (£3.99)

Hong Kong Heroic Bloodshed (£2.99)

Slasher Movies(£3.99)

Vampire Films (£2.99)

Film Subjects:

Laurel & Hardy (£3.99)

Steve McQueen (£2.99)

The Oscars® (£3.99)

Bruce Lee (£3.99)

Marx Brothers (£3.99)

Marilyn Monroe (£3.99)

Filming On A Microbudget (£3.99)

Film Music (£3.99)

TV:

Doctor Who (£3.99)

Literature:

Cyberpunk (£3.99)

Hitchhiker's Guide (£3.99)

Terry Pratchett (£3.99)

Philip K Dick (£3.99)

Noir Fiction (£2.99)

Sherlock Holmes (£3.99)

Ideas:

Conspiracy Theories (£3.99)

Feminism (£3.99)

Nietzsche (£3.99)

History:

Alchemy & Alchemists (£3.99)

American Civl War (£3.99)

The Crusades (£3.99)

American Indian Wars (£3.99)

Available at all good bookstores, or send a cheque to: **Pocket Essentials (Dept MH), 18 Coleswood Rd, Harpenden, Herts, AL5 1EQ, UK**. Please make cheques payable to 'Oldcastle Books.' Add 50p postage & packing for each book in the UK and £1 elsewhere.

US customers can send $6.95 plus $1.95 postage & packing for each book to: **Trafalgar Square Publishing, PO Box 257, Howe Hill Road, North Pomfret, Vermont 05053, USA**. e-mail: tsquare@sover.net

Customers worldwide can order online at **www.pocketessentials.com**.

The Essential Library

Build up your library with new titles every month

Agatha Christie by Mark Campbell, £3.99

Foreword by Simon Brett. Since her debut in 1920 with The Mysterious Affair At Styles, Agatha Christie has become the chief proponent of the English village murder mystery. She created two enormously popular characters - the Belgian detective Hercule Poirot, and the inquisitive elderly spinster and amateur sleuth Miss Jane Marple of St Mary Mead – and wrote in many different genres.

As well as an informed introduction to the Christie phenomenon, this book examines all her novels and short stories. The film, TV and stage adaptations are listed, and the appendices point you to books and websites where you can find out more.

French New Wave by Chris Wiegand, £3.99

The directors of the French New Wave were the original film geeks - a collection of celluloid-crazed cinéphiles with a background in film criticism and a love for American auteurs. Having spent countless hours slumped in Parisian cinémathèques, they armed themselves with handheld cameras, rejected conventions, and successfully moved movies out of the studios and on to the streets at the end of the 1950s.

Borrowing liberally from the varied traditions of film noir, musicals and science fiction, they released a string of innovative and influential pictures, including the classics Le Beau Serge, Jules Et Jim and A Bout De Souffle. By the mid-1960s, the likes of Jean-Luc Godard, François Truffaut, Claude Chabrol, Louis Malle, Eric Rohmer and Alain Resnais had changed the rules of film-making forever.

Bollywood by Ashok Banker, £3.99

Bombay's prolific Hindi-language film industry is more than just a giant entertainment juggernaut for 1 billion-plus Indians worldwide. It's a part of Indian culture, language, fashion and lifestyle. It's also a great bundle of contradictions and contrasts, like India itself. Thrillers, horror, murder mysteries, courtroom dramas, Hong Kong-style action gunfests, romantic comedies, soap operas, mythological costume dramas... they're all blended with surprising skill into the musical boy-meets-girl formula of Bollywood. The results are a bizarre, overblown mixture of high concept, ethnic colour, traditional values, high-pitched emotional drama, sizzling sensuality and music, always music.

This vivid introduction to Bollywood, written by a Bollywood scriptwriter and media commentator, examines 50 major films in entertaining and intimate detail.

The Hitchhiker's Guide by MJ Simpson, £3.99

Updated Edition. Foreword by Simon Jones. Based on 20 years of research and extensive interviews with the cast and crew of Hitchhiker's Guide, including the late Douglas Adams, this book also includes details of Douglas Adams' other projects (Dirk Gently, The Meaning Of Liff and Starship Titanic) plus his early work on series such as Doctor Who and Monty Python's Flying Circus.

Available at all good bookstores, or send a cheque to: **Pocket Essentials (Dept MH), 18 Coleswood Rd, Harpenden, Herts, AL5 1EQ, UK**. Please make cheques payable to 'Oldcastle Books.' Add 50p postage & packing for each book in the UK and £1 elsewhere.

US customers can send $6.95 plus $1.95 postage & packing for each book to: **Trafalgar Square Publishing, PO Box 257, Howe Hill Road, North Pomfret, Vermont 05053, USA**. e-mail: tsquare@sover.net

Customers worldwide can order online at **www.pocketessentials.com**.